King Solomon showed us that no matter how successful we may be in the world's eyes we will fail in our use of money if we do not have a foundation on God. Shane provides the practical tools but also a Biblical foundation for teaching your children about money.

-Dr. Greg Smalley
Author of *The Wholehearted Marriage*

Research shows that what parents teach and model in the home is more influential, as much as two to three times more influential, than any church program. The Bible clearly depicts (Deuteronomy 6, Joshua 24) that the home is the primary place where faith is to be nurtured with the church serving as a life-long partner, not replacement, that is continually equipping parents to know, tell and be the Christian story with their children in their homes. Dad Cents is an inspirational yet practical faith@home resource that helps parents know, tell and be what they need to know, tell and be regarding God's approach to money.

-Pastor Mark Holmen
Author, Speaker, Ministry Coach and full-time Missionary for the Faith@Home Movement

Many dads, make that most dads, struggle with how to teach their children about handling the resources God brings their way. My friend, Shane Barkley, has done families everywhere a huge favor. This book will challenge your old assumptions about money.

-Dr. Paul Pettit
President & Founder
Dynamic Dads
Dallas, Texas.

D1113794

Financial problems are a major cause of marital distress and create havoc in many lives. One of the greatest gifts we can give to our children that will stand them in good stead throughout their lives is how to be good stewards of God's many gifts—especially our financial resources. Tragically this is an area in which many well-meaning parents fail. Shane's book is an invaluable gift to every dad (and mom) who want their children to have practical and biblically-based principles and tools to help them develop the skills they'll need to be faithful stewards throughout their lives and enjoy greater personal and professional success.

-Gary J. Oliver, Ph.D.,
Author of *Mad About Us* and Executive Director of The Center for Relationship Enrichment and Professor of Psychology and Practical Theology at John Brown University.

Though I was very young, I clearly remember when my dad started giving me an allowance. He taped three little boxes together. On one he wrote "Church," on the second he wrote "Savings," and on the third he wrote "Spending." Then he gave me three nickels—one for each box. He started simple and small, but my dad's early instruction on managing money has influenced me all my life. In similarly practical ways, this book can help dads influence their children's views about and uses of money to the glory of God.

-Dr. Donald S. Whitney
Author of *Spiritual Disciplines for the Christian Life*, founder and president of The Center for Biblical Spirituality, Associate Professor of Biblical Spirituality and Senior Associate Dean at The Southern Baptist Theological Seminary in Louisville, Kentucky.

Money and material possessions influence many areas of life, and having the right perspective in this area can be a huge head start for your children. This book provides a winning game plan and practical tools to help you equip them to be good stewards, and along the way you'll all be challenged to be more devoted followers of Christ.

-Carey Casey
CEO, National Center for Fathering – fathers.com
Author, *Championship Fathering*

Dad Cents builds a solid Biblical foundation for your family's finances, and delivers easy to reach, practical guidance for sharing it with kids of all ages.

-Joe White
President of Kanakuk Kamps

I will be recommending DAD CENTS to fathers I coach and dads I speak to. It provides a simple blueprint to build a solid foundation for Biblical family finances. I appreciate the practical daily steps to "Do The Work" and the age-appropriate tips for training your kids at each stage about wise money management.

-Timothy Smith
Author, speaker, family coach, and President of ParentsCoach.org

dad ¢ents

TEACH YOUR CHILDREN BIBLICAL PRINCIPLES OF MONEY

SHANE BARKLEY

Cover photo by: MattMasonPhotography.com
Cover design by: Julie Nor - Flairstudio.net
Printing by Hall Commercial Printing

DAD CENTS

ISBN: 978-0-9818902-1-0

Timothy Publishing is proud to provide publishing services in cooperation with Shane Barkley, Author of Dad Cents: Teach Your Children Biblical Principles of Money. All rights and obligations are solely held by the Author.

Timothy Publishing
1353 Lake Shore Drive
Branson Mo 65616

Timothy Publishing is a division of Kanakuk Ministries dba Kanakuk Kamps. Each year Kanakuk Kamps serves as the summer home to more than 14,000 kids from across the globe.

Kanakuk Kamps
Exciting Adventure in Christian Athletics.

www.kanakuk.com

Table of Contents

Do

Secret

Table of Contents

Foreword

Ken R. Canfield, Ph.D.

Let me start by saying you've done your children (and likely your grandchildren) a great service by picking up this book. If your kids are still pretty young and they're many years away from being gainfully employed, it may not seem vital to teach them about money. But a quick look at the head-lines—about the size of our national debt, the unpredictable state of our economy, and the irresponsibility that has helped to bring us to this point—will likely convince you that money truly is (and will continue to be) a huge topic for our families and children, and it's never too early to start teaching them.

Or, perhaps I should say, it's never too early to start being in-tentional in what we're teaching them. I believe that, as fathers, we're always teaching through our modeling. Our children are watching us and learning from us whether or not we realize it, and whether or not we're setting a positive example for them.

Look at the people around you. Marriages and households are stressed by the pressures of bill collectors or they may have ongoing conflict because spouses can't agree on what to do with their money. Many young adults enter the workforce carrying a mountain of debt already, and few of them have the skills or the wisdom to know how to remedy the situation. Dads get laid off and have no savings to fall back on until they can find another job and consequently put their families into debt so deep that it takes years to recover.

Our society revolves around money, and a lot of the evidence says that it's spinning out of control. As fathers, we need to talk with our children about money, and model the right attitude about it. Our goal is not to frighten them, but to help them gain a positive outlook about money, and to teach them healthy stewardship habits. Those seem like obvious action steps, but few fathers are actually doing it. If we want to save our children from the agony of worshipping the almighty dollar, we need to make it a priority to help them put money in the proper perspective.

Much of my research on fatherhood has focused on the "life course" of fathers. It's based on the premise that fathers need to adapt to their children's changing needs as the children go through the different stages of childhood—and as fathers go through their own changes as adults.

Looking at fatherhood from this perspective has a few distinct advantages: For one, it helps dads better understand the stage they are currently going through and better meet the needs of their children during that phase of life. A father's role when his children are toddlers will be much different from his role when they're in grade school or when they are teenagers. (If his role isn't any different, then he isn't a very involved father.)

Along with that, the life course allows us to take a step back from our current challenges and see the bigger picture of our fatherhood. We can see how our teenager has changed in the past ten years, and hold out hope that the fun, more agreeable kid we knew at age eight will return in a few years. Or we can drop off our child for her first day of school and know that we need to start planning for the many other ways she'll express her growing independence in the coming years. That larger perspective helps us keep an eye a few miles down the road ahead of where we are now, and reminds us that our role is always growing and changing.

Of course, the life course approach is also useful as we think about training our children to be good stewards of money. That's one reason the Dad Cents approach makes so much sense to me. Thinking back, I could have done a much better job in this arena and I would have benefitted immensely from the ideas that Shane has collected in his book.

Shane provides a solid foundation for dads of young children, and equips them to teach sound principles that those children need. Then, dads of elementary kids and tweeners will find insights on the topics and issues that they are sure to face. It's all part of the process of training kids to make wise choices with money once they're out on their own, and Shane's chapter for dads of teenagers offers sound guidance to help complete that process. There are practical, useful nuggets for dads at every stage along the way.

Another reason this book is important: to my knowledge, it holds a unique place in the landscape of resources on similar topics. You can find books on financial management written from a Biblical perspective, and you can find books to help you train your children to handle money. Shane has combined those two characteristics, and that makes this book especially relevant and useful. Money is too important a topic to be handled without consulting divine wisdom at every turn.

The Bible urges us to store up treasures not on earth, but rather in heaven. I believe that when we turn our hearts to our children, we are stockpiling great treasures in the eyes of God. And He will—as our father—return great treasures back to us, whether they are financial or, even better, relational.

I appreciate Shane's simple and direct approach to stewardship. Even though his children are still in the home, he's gleaned insights from the world of finance (via his training and vocational background) and presents them in a manner that will help you. He's a committed husband to Val, a father to three beautiful daughters and a brother in the Lord.

The topic may be money, but the goal is bonding with your children and investing more of yourself in them. If any book can do that—and I believe this one can— then I'm all in!

Introduction

We have a neighbor who's a pilot for the Air National Guard. Sometimes, when he returns from a trip to a far-off part of the world, he'll bring back foreign currency to give to my oldest daughter, Jerica. She has money from Asia, Europe, Central America, the Middle East and Australia, and she loves to look at the different colors, pictures, and writing on each piece of currency.

To my daughter, those coins and bills are like play money. But to me, a dad who has almost ten years of experience in the financial consulting field, I view that money as a teaching opportunity. I'm eager to explain to her how the value of that money translates to American dollars (or, more likely, dimes and nickels), but it's a real challenge. Somehow, the concept of exchange rates just doesn't translate well to her level of understanding.

And sure, I could try harder. I could lay out dollars next to the foreign currency so she could get a better idea how it compares. That would make for a good math problem some day.

But as I think about this, I realize that a lesson in exchange rates isn't even in the ballpark of what I really want my daughter to learn about money. As soon as I use a word like "worth" or "value" with her, I know those words carry much deeper meaning, far beyond being able to count currency or do math computations.

That illustrates the basic question I'll be addressing in this book. It's a big question that you need to answer and then act upon: What do you want for your children when it comes to money?

I'm asking that question with a long-range perspective in mind. After all, the end goal of our fathering efforts is to send out a young adult into the world who's responsible, content, and able to manage his or her finances wisely.

We know that money will be such a big part of our children's lives. Through good stewardship, money can bring them many positive opportunities to please God and enjoy His blessings; and poor stewardship can become a stumbling block that closes doors for them or keeps them from becoming all God has called them to be.

From what I have seen and heard, most fathers don't often consider the importance of financial training for their children's future. I have asked dads, "When your kids leave home and begin life on their own, do you want their financial knowledge to be worse than, the same as, or better than yours when you left home?" Without hesitation, every dad expressed that he wants his children to know more than he did when he left home. But then he'll often follow that with a comment like, "But I don't know if that will happen."

Few of us have experienced much useful teaching of financial principles from one generation to the next, and that makes it even more difficult to start with our children. I have asked large groups of men if they are currently using any financial teaching they received from their parents. From a recent sample of about 400 men, only four of them raised their hands! And it's been my experience that the teaching that those few people did receive from their parents was almost all secular in nature and not Biblical.

God's Word has a lot to say about the stewardship of money, and passing on that wisdom to our children has become a lost art. I believe that's the number one reason why many dads today need this book—to have foundational principles and practical ideas that will help them succeed in preparing their children to be good stewards as adults.

Beyond that, it doesn't take more than a quick look at our culture to find more reasons why people need a tool like this.

As a financial consultant, I worked with a wide range of individuals who had various levels of assets, income, and knowledge. But most of their stories followed a common theme: they knew they should be planning for the future and saving money every month, but they were not doing so. A few people faced a string of emergencies that required large chunks of their money, but most often, they couldn't resist spending their money on things they wanted to acquire. Those desires they saw today outweighed the unknown of the future. Many of them didn't know sound, Biblical principles of stewardship; the ones who did have the knowledge usually didn't have the willpower to put that knowledge into practice.

Most of us are very familiar with the cultural forces that are working against good financial stewardship. For example, few people today are equipped to look at advertising and other available consumer information, see it for what it really is, and make wise decisions. What is that commercial really promising? And how ridiculous is it to think the product can really deliver on that promise? Does drinking beer really help men attract beautiful women? Can driving a luxury car really transform me into someone "cool"? We see those ads promise something they can't deliver, and yet our culture is filled with people who are buying into those empty promises—and the financial consequences that come with them.

There is so much information and misinformation in the

world today, and knowing what is accurate, reliable and trust-worthy is becoming more and more difficult. Adults every-where are buying into the lies, so how can children help but follow? There's no one training them to evaluate the messages they hear and make wise choices.

Of course, this trend has contributed to the debt culture that is so prevalent in recent years. We are a country of debt-ors following the lead of our government. So deficit spending and living beyond our means has become the norm in fami-lies, businesses, and just about everywhere else we look. The cost of our desires outweighs the cash in the bank, and we continue to mortgage our future.

One powerful example showed up in a 2008 report on col-lege students and credit card use. It's no wonder that students are prime targets for credit card companies when "forty-four percent carry forward a balance each billing period, with an average outstanding balance of more than $2,000." And debt from college expenses continues to rise. "Graduating seniors in the Class of 2006 left college with an average debt estimat-ed at $21,000 in educational loan obligations, an 8 percent increase over average student loan debt in just the previous year."[1]

That's no way to start out in the world after college, and as fathers, we can do a lot to help our children avoid that trap and others like it. No matter what age your children are, you can start teaching sound principles and giving them real-life experiences that will help your children be more responsible with their money.

Again, I'll ask you that big question: What do you want for your children when it comes to money? And then, what steps are you taking to educate your children financially? If you're like many of the fathers and families I see, you aren't prepar-ing your children like you could be.

Introduction

As you can probably tell, this subject is something I'm very passionate about. I believe fathers are a big part of the solution to many of the disturbing trends in our society, and they can pass on so many key values to their children through these money principles, if they are equipped and motivated to do so. I have lots of experience with these concepts, and I've seen them work in families. I have a degree in business and ten years of experience in the financial consulting field, but more than that, I'm a dad and a follower of Jesus. This is a calling that God has placed on my life. I believe you can make a difference for your children and generations to come, and I'm confident that I can help you.

If you want to be part of that, then this book is for you.

Chapter 1
What's Your Foundation?

"... like a skilled master-builder I laid a foundation, but someone else builds on it. And each one must be careful how he builds. For no one can lay any foundation other than what is being laid, which is Jesus Christ. If anyone builds on the foundation with gold, silver, precious stones, wood, hay, or straw, each builder's work will be plainly seen ..." 1 Corinthians 3:10-13

Imagine you are looking at the plans for your dream house. The blueprints have been drawn to your exact specifications, and it's everything your wife has ever wanted in a house. You chose just the right builder for the project, and he is crafting it as if he were building for the President. The best subcontractors in the area are on board. An interior decorator is ready to match colors, fixtures, carpet and trim to your desired effect. The land is in a secluded area that you happened to find by word of mouth, and it was surprisingly affordable. You and your wife have been planning for this for a long time.

On the third day of construction, the two of you manage to drop by to check things out, and as you pull up, you cannot believe your eyes. They already have the decking in place for the roof! It's certainly beautiful, but your excitement quickly fades when you get closer and discover that your builder has erected the roof first, before digging down and pouring concrete for the foundation. (Clearly, he wasn't the right builder after all.)

As crazy and unlikely as this story might sound, it's an appropriate way to describe how too many people today approach their finances. They're trying to live in a mansion that has no foundation. They don't have important values and principles in place that will guide their decisions and help them teach their children.

Maybe a better example is the people who build houses on the sides of hills or mountains. The views are beautiful, but the foundations are not secure. Due to mudslides or the gradual pull of gravity, many of these houses eventually start slipping down the mountain. Engineers warn of the inherent danger of building in such risky locations, but people do it anyway. The homeowner is more concerned about the view and they don't understand the vital importance of a firm foundation.

It's no accident that the financial world speaks of building wealth, building your future and building a business. Buildings require a strong foundation. That's a necessary first step. Anything built without a proper foundation will surely fail. Many people are making financial decisions without having a strong foundation in place. There are many different expressions of the problem, but the core issue is that people are living for and pursuing what they desire today, even if it means piling up huge amounts of debt, with little regard for the future.

There are other people whom we would think of as more responsible with their money. They do plan, save and invest wisely, and are well prepared for future needs that may arise. But if the end goal is simply their own pleasure, or comfort, or a sense that they are "secure," that still isn't a strong, reliable foundation. Though they may have few financial worries right now, their foundation could crumble with a job loss, health problems or a natural disaster. Very quickly, more important things will emerge, such as having a strong marriage, having close connections with their kids, and living in a way that will leave a Godly legacy when they're gone.

Money may not be the whole picture, but it's a key part of the picture, because so much of our true character and priorities show up in our money management. If we take our financial stewardship seriously and do our best to stay close to God's purposes in that area, those positive values and purposes will influence other key areas of our lives as well.

Who's Watching You?

How often have you heard parents—whether your parents, other people you know or even yourself—tell a child, "Do what I say, not what I do"? I can understand what those parents are thinking in the moment. They realize that they aren't perfect, and they want something better for their children. They want their children to overcome some of the challenges and shortcomings they see in their own lives.

But I'm really concerned when I hear that—and you probably share those concerns—because the parent is basically telling his child, "I expect something of you that I don't really take that seriously myself." So, for example, that parent might talk about honesty and integrity, but then will use a radar detector in his car. Or he'll say, "The car doesn't move until your seatbelts are on," but then he doesn't fasten his own until he sees a police officer.

The truth is, we can talk 'til we're blue in the face, but the people close to us know what we really stand for, and that's communicated mostly through our actions. They know what kind of ground we've used to build the foundation for our house. It's reflected in the daily decisions we make with our time, energy and money.

My friends at the National Center for Fathering (fathers. com) tell the story about Bruce, who was treating his three kids and himself to an all-you-can-eat pizza buffet. From the outside, they couldn't miss the buffet prices painted in huge numbers and bright colors on the window: $4.49 for adults and $2.49 for kids age 4 to 9.

Since Bruce's oldest child, Parker, had just celebrated his 10th birthday, he noticed the sign and commented on it as they stood in line to pay. He was a little bit proud that he'd be charged the full price for his pizza. Bruce, of course, wasn't so thrilled.

When they reached the cashier, she didn't ask how old Parker was, and Bruce didn't say anything. She quickly rang up one adult and three children, Bruce paid the money, and they were herded through.

It was a simple oversight, except that Parker is one of those kids who notices everything. So when they sat down, he pointed it out. "Dad, they didn't charge us enough, did they?" Suddenly it was very clear to Bruce that he should have paid more attention to that transaction—because it was the right thing to do, and because his son was watching to see how he handled it. "You're right, son," he said, and immediately he went back and paid the difference.

The girl at the register tried to wave him off and say it didn't matter; it was only a few dollars. But to Bruce, it did matter. His integrity was on the line—at least in the eyes of his children. He did the right thing eventually, but he knows he should have done it right the first time. Bruce realizes that those everyday interactions are teaching opportunities, and his children will be powerfully influenced by their memories of him, whether he relaxed his standards and compromised godly values, or he went out of his way to do the right thing.

I am amazed at how perceptive kids are, even at a young age. At our house, we regularly take toys and clothing to the local rescue mission. Every time my wife packs a box to be taken to the mission, she explains to our three young girls what she's doing and why.

I'll never forget May of 2007, when a tornado ripped through the town of Greensburg, right here in Kansas. It registered a F5 on the Fujita scale, meaning the winds were in excess of 200 m.p.h., and cut a path as big as 1½ miles wide for about 20 miles. The tornado reduced to ruins pretty much everything in that path, including the town of Greensburg. We're used to the threat of tornados every spring and summer, but we rarely hear about a tornado of that magnitude.

As we watched the coverage on television with the rest of the nation, we tried to explain to our oldest daughter, Jerica, what had happened and the devastation that had occurred. She promptly asked my wife for a box. "Why do you need a box?" my wife asked. She replied, "We need to give some of our toys and clothes to the kids who lost theirs." At just 5 years old, thanks to my wife's modeling, Jerica understood that people need help and God has equipped us to help. Needless to say, my wife and I were astounded and nearly brought to tears by her actions.

I hope you agree with Bruce and me that it's worth a little money—no, it's worth a lot of money—to demonstrate integrity and be a positive model for our kids. We must remember that they're always watching us, always taking mental notes about decisions we make and how we respond in certain situations. They're depending on us not only to draw boundaries for them about what's right and wrong, but also to reinforce those boundaries with our actions.

Once again, modeling honesty and integrity should apply to all areas of our fathering, but money and possessions are often involved in those opportunities. And we know that the Bible mentions the subject of money more than any other topic—prayer, salvation, worship, anything! So it's clear that God knows the tremendous effect that money has on our lives.

Rock or Sand?

It's interesting that Jesus also talked about *building* and *foundations*, and His words apply well to this important first step in thinking about money. The well-known passage from Matthew chapter seven makes it clear that people who hear Jesus' words and put them into practice are like a man who built his house on a rock. People who do not adopt Jesus' principles for life are building on sand. The house on the firm foundation—the rock—withstands storms and high water, but the house built on sand falls with a great crash (vv. 24-27).

The best way to build a foundation is with an eye on the eternal. That's the only foundation that is truly secure. The end result is about more than acquiring possessions, accumulating wealth, or gaining approval from the world. Money is a tool that God has given us to achieve His purposes—that's our end result.

Paul addresses this question in his first letter to Timothy. He describes "people corrupted in their minds and deprived of the truth, who suppose that godliness is a way of making a profit. Now," he continues, "*godliness combined with contentment brings great profit. *For we have brought nothing into this world and so we cannot take a single thing out either. But if we have food and shelter, we will be satisfied with that. Those who long to be rich, however, stumble into temptation and a trap and many senseless and harmful desires that plunge people into ruin and destruction. For the love of money is the root of all evils. Some people in reaching for it have strayed from the faith and stabbed themselves with many pains." (6:5-10, emphasis added).

During all the years I spent in the world of financial consulting, I learned a lot of mainstream financial concepts and strategies for planning, saving, investing, and many other great ideas. Even when I did encounter people who were doing those things wisely, I always sensed that something was missing for them. They weren't truly fulfilled or content. I'm convinced that what most of them were missing was a deeper purpose. Their foundation was not the Solid Rock of Jesus Christ.

First Corinthians 3:11 tells us plainly, "For no one can lay any foundation other than what is being laid, which is Jesus Christ." True life—abundant life—begins with that recognition. Are you living with a strong sense of accountability to God for how you steward His money? Are you seeking to gain approval from Him more than others? If so, that will guide you to be a good money manager and a committed father who teaches your children—and models for them—what it means to have a foundation that cannot be shaken.

Have you submitted your whole life to Jesus? If you haven't and you'd like to learn more, please turn to the appendix at the back of the book entitled, "Eternal Matters."

The Richest Man Ever

What if I told you that there's a new Forbes World Billionaires list that has just been published, and a new entrepreneur has broken through to the top of the list? The information we have about his assets and annual income paints a picture that is quite astonishing.

His annual income is estimated to be just over $522 million. Yes, that's *annually*! His land holdings amount to about 7.7 million acres. At a mere $5,000 per acre, that adds up to $38.4 billion. He also owns significant property on that land— magnificent houses, ranches, and about 12,000 horses and other livestock. There is a rumor that he donated 22,000 head of cattle and over 120,000 sheep and goats several years ago. He also has a fleet of ships and about 1,400 cars.

If you're like me, you want to hear the rest of the story about this guy. Actually, that description is an estimate in today's values of the assets of King Solomon as described in the book of 1 Kings.

When we think of King Solomon, we think of him as one of the wealthiest men ever, but we also remember him for being one of the wisest. Try to put yourself in his shoes in 1 Kings chapter 3, when God came to him and said, "Tell me what I should give you." Even on my most clear-headed and noble-minded days, I have a hard time believing I would respond as Solomon did. He humbled himself, referred to himself as a "young man," and asked God for a discerning mind to govern God's people and distinguish right from wrong.

As you know, God was pleased with that response, and He gave Solomon what he asked for—and then some. He gave him great wisdom *and* great wealth. God told him he would have "a wise and discerning mind superior to that of anyone who has preceded or will succeed you." Solomon proved that wisdom and wealth can be a great combination if used properly.

For many years of his life, the foundation of Solomon's life was his heavenly Father, and he prospered in every way. But like so many people, he grew complacent, too comfortable or too self-sufficient. Later in life, even with all his wisdom, he allowed himself to be led astray by his foreign wives and their gods. Maybe he grew too comfortable with his wealth and he stopped relying completely on God. He made important com-promises and it led to hard times.

In 1 Kings 11:11, God told Solomon, "Because you insist on doing these things and have not kept the covenantal rules I gave you, I will surely tear the kingdom away from you and give it to your servant."

King Solomon is proof that you can be wealthy beyond measure and have great wisdom as well, but if your foundation isn't built on the rock of God's Word—and the Word that later became flesh, Jesus Christ—and if you don't maintain that solid foundation, then you won't be truly satisfied in life. True success is not found in the amount of money you have in the bank, but in pursuing God's vision for your life to the point that you're keeping His commandments.

Teaching Adults

Are you building your house on the rock or the sand? Since we are going to be focusing on finances, I will ask again, "Are you building your financial house on the rock of God or the sand of worldly wisdom?"

Here's the key question you need to consider: *What do you want for your children when it comes to money, how they define "success," and their ability to find true contentment in life?*

If your children are young like mine, the answer may be difficult for you to imagine. But right now you're helping them build a foundation for their entire lives. Remember, parenting is about investing ourselves in people who will one day become adults. The goal of your fathering is a responsible 19-to-22-year-old who will one day leave your protective covering. What will his response be when the storms of adversity hit and he faces tough decisions? You and I want godly decisions to come out of our children, especially when money is a part of the storm they are facing.

None of us would ever wish hard times on our children, but I have also seen how wealth can bring its own set of challenges and hard times. Like Jesus said, "It is easier for a camel to go through the eye of a needle than for a rich person to enter into the kingdom of God" (Matt. 19:24). And who's to say what makes a person "rich"? It's a relative term. Am I rich in comparison to Donald Trump? *No.* What about compared to the average person in a third-world country? *Well, that's different.* It all depends on your perspective.

In the end, no matter how much my children have in terms

of wealth and material possessions, I want them to learn important lessons about money and life by working through some challenges, learning to work hard and get by on what they earn, and most of all, learning to trust in God for everything and keep their foundation built on Christ.

Throughout this book, I will provide you with practical information I am using to teach my girls about money. First and foremost, I will explore some key principles of God's truth about money. That's the most important part of the foundation—maybe the cornerstone, if you will. The real power of what you teach your children will stand or fall based on whether you are firmly grounded in the Word.

I will include some insights that don't come directly from God's Word, but that are consistent with Biblical teachings on money. I will do my best to make it clear how those "worldly" insights can be viewed as expressions of Biblical principles.

Now, let's start building on that foundation.

Chapter 2

The DADS Approach

"Now Ezra had dedicated himself to the study of the law of the Lord, to its observance, and to teaching its statutes and judgments in Israel."
Ezra 7:10

Now that the foundation is in place, it's time to start setting some of the structure on top of it. The next section of the book is what I am calling the "DADS" approach. There are about a dozen principles, habits, and character qualities from scripture that I will highlight. All Christian dads need to grasp these and keep them in mind as they teach their children about money.

Ultimately, these are important for all of us to teach to our children. But since we can't teach what we don't grasp—we can't give away what we don't have—the first step is making sure we're all on the same page with these things. I'm confident that a few concepts in this section will be new territory for at least some dads. So, you might need to contemplate and test some of this in your own money management before you will be ready to teach it to your children.

Before getting into the meat of these chapters, I want to give you the big picture, the whole structure of the DADS approach:

D: **D**iscover the Truth
A: Be an **A**dvocate
D: **D**o the Work
S: Learn the **S**ecret

The first **D** is for **Discover the Truth**. All our dealings with money and possessions must begin with a few key concepts from God's Word. When it comes to money, what is our God-given role, and what does He expect of us?

A stands for **Advocate**. Grasping and embracing God's truth about money should change us. It should motivate us to develop character traits in our children that line up with His will for us, and those traits will lead us to ...

D: **Do** the work on a day-to-day basis. Our understanding and our inner virtues must lead us to God-honoring actions. We don't merely read about wise money management; we live it out.

The D-A-D part of this approach echoes the verse from Ezra that I used at the beginning of this chapter, though the order is different. Like Ezra, we are to dedicate ourselves to studying God's Word about money (Discover), observing it or living it out in everyday life (Do), and teaching it to our children (Advocate).

If we are faithful in those ways when it comes to money, that leads to the **S**: Paul mentions a **Secret** in Philippians that is a great benefit for those who discover, advocate, and do. In a sense, this secret is like a reward for us, but it also feeds a desire to go deeper with the previous steps. (Stay tuned for a lot more on this secret.)

I hope this acrostic provides an easy way for you to remember these important concepts related to money. God's Word is the foundation we need to guide our thoughts and actions for our children's benefit.

Chapter 3

Discover the Truth: Ownership

"The Lord owns the earth and all it contains, the world and all who live in it." Psalm 24:1

Several years ago, my wife and I had the privilege of working on the crew for one of the *Extreme Makeover: Home Edition* houses in Chapman, Kansas. It was hard work, but a fun and very rewarding experience. In a similar way, we're going to go through an *Extreme Mind Makeover: God Edition* here. But don't worry, I can assure you that this too will be a rewarding experience.

The first step in the D.A.D.S. approach—Discover the Truth—involves establishing the basic truth about the world of money and possessions. We'll start with the concept of ownership. This is a funny concept in our world.

Ownership is nine-tenths of the law, right?
"How do you like *my* new car?" we ask our friends.
"*He* owns two successful companies."
Politicians talk about letting us keep more of *our* money.
"Nobody's gonna tell me what to do with *my* stuff!"
"Come over and watch the game on *our* big screen."
"Put *your* money in a tax shelter," experts advise us.
"I'm keeping a close eye on *my* investments."

"I'm still paying on *my* mortgage, but *I own* over sixty percent of my house."

We hear these kinds of statements all the time. And yet, in reality, we really only have a *sense* of ownership with any of them. Ownership is an illusion more than anything else. Any of these things could break, burn up, or lose all their value in a matter of moments, and the illusion of ownership would be over. We actually don't control much of what happens with them. The fact that we can even maintain the illusion of ownership is a blessing from God.

Do you own your possessions? It may seem like you do, but I would advise you to shatter that illusion right now. It is misguided and, frankly, a bit dangerous. Several places in Scripture clearly show that God is the owner of everything. Really. Everything! Psalm 24:1 tells us, "The Lord owns the earth and all it contains, the world and all who live in it." We don't even own ourselves! And in Job 41:11, God says to Job, "Who has confronted me that I should repay? Everything under heaven belongs to me!"

Claiming ownership is almost like trying to take what is rightfully God's or presuming to play God in our own lives—and we're no match for Him. We'd be much wiser to acknowledge His rightful position, His lordship in our lives, His ownership of everything, and then figure out how we fit into the equation.

But too often, we can't get past all the stuff in the world around us and the prevailing attitudes in the culture that pressure us. We grow dissatisfied with what we have, spend money based on present desires more than long-term goals or needs, and even find our self-worth in some worldly definition of "success"—not God's definition. It doesn't take a huge error to get us off track.

So often, that's how it is in the Christian life: over time, even small errors can lead us way off course. I can be moving in a direction that's one degree off the true north that God wants for me, and for quite a while it will seem like I'm just a step or two from where I need to be. But if I continue on that course without making a correction, eventually I'm hundreds of miles off course. If I set out to fly from Kansas to Florida and my navigating equipment is off even by a degree, chances are I won't end up at Disney World.

So it is with God's truth and our thinking about money. Seeking to fit in with those around us, we might make small, almost imperceptible concessions day by day until we turn around one day and see that we've missed out on the best that God wants for us, and some major backtracking will need to happen in order to get back in step with Him.

As Christians, we may think we have this one covered. Money and stuff will never master us, right? Then along comes a recession, or we go through a divorce or some other huge challenge that affects our bank balance, and suddenly we become much more sticky-fingered about what's ours and what we see as God's. We aren't willing to make sacrifices or skip creature comforts for ourselves, even for kingdom causes. In hard times, so often our tithe is among the first budget items that we skip, but we keep our cable TV and refuse to cut back on eating out or seeing movies.

Now, you may be asking, "All these results can arise from our perception of ownership?" Yes, they can. When we fail to grasp the basic truth or fail to live with the awareness that "the Lord owns the earth and all it contains," we are setting a course that will eventually lead us hundreds or even thousands of miles from where we want to be, which is also far from experiencing the fullness of God's blessings. And experiencing this fullness begins with each of us placing God on the throne of our lives and letting Him be God, the Creator and Owner, the loving Father who wants to teach us and teach our children more about who He is.

Now, what's our proper place as we stand before His throne? If God is the owner of everything we have, then what relationship do we have with the possessions that we control? Read on to discover one more essential truth.

Chapter 4

Discover the Truth: Stewardship

"From everyone who has been given much, much will be required, and from the one who has been entrusted with much, even more will be asked."   Luke 12:48b

This second big truth flows straight out of the first. If God is the owner of everything, then we are to be stewards—managers of what He has entrusted to us. Sometimes, "steward" is translated as "slave."

There really is a shift in thinking that has to take place as we discover and come to understand our role. During my years in the financial consulting field, I gained some new first-hand experiences with this. I was put in charge of managing other people's money and, I can assure you, it made me think twice about decisions I made on the owners' behalf. Because they were paying me to do a good job, I felt a strong sense of accountability to them, and I gave my best effort. I did whatever it took to help them make the most of their money.

With that in mind, how much more should I be thoughtful and wise about how I manage what God has placed in my care? He is the ultimate Owner, and I know I should feel an even stronger sense of accountability to Him. I should seek to do my very best. Sometimes it's harder to maintain that perspective with God since He doesn't regularly call me on the phone or physically stop by my office to ask how I'm doing with His resources. But I strive to live with the awareness that He is my loving Father, my ever-present King, who expects me to utilize and multiply His resources and use them for His ultimate glory.

The Bible makes this plain in the parable Jesus told that is recorded in Luke 19. The owner trusts varying amounts of money to three servants, and he rewards them based on how they managed that money and whether they multiplied the original amount. The owner, representing God, rewards those servants who invested the money wisely and increased it, and he reprimands the one servant who merely hid the money to keep it safe. I'll look at this parable again a few chapters later. For now, we need to understand that being a steward is a serious responsibility.

In another parable, Jesus told his disciples, "Get dressed for service and keep your lamps burning; be like people waiting for their master to come back from the wedding celebration, so that when he comes and knocks they can immediately open the door for him. Blessed are those slaves whom their master finds alert when he returns! I tell you the truth, he will dress himself to serve, have them take their place at the table, and will come and wait on them!" (Luke 12:35-37). Several verses later, Jesus explains further:

> Who then is the faithful and wise manager, whom the master puts in charge of his household servants, to give them their allowance of food at the proper time? Blessed is that slave whom his master finds at work when he returns. I tell you the truth, the master will put him in charge of all his possessions. But if that slave should say to himself, "My master is de-

layed in returning," and he begins to beat the other slaves, both men and women, and to eat, drink, and get drunk, then the master of that slave will come on a day when he does not expect him and at an hour he does not foresee, and will cut him in two, and assign him a place with the unfaithful. (vv. 42-46)

Jesus gives us a clear picture of what it takes to be a good steward. We are to be faithful, wise, and attentive. We should always be "alert" to determine how we might please God with His resources in a given situation. We should be ever mindful that we will be held accountable for how we manage the Master's possessions. "From everyone who has been given much," Jesus says, "much will be required, and from the one who has been entrusted with much, even more will be asked" (48b).

Stewards with Vision

So, if God owns everything, how should we treat everything? Does the phrase "It's a rental" ring a bell? Actually, knowing the way some apartment tenants treat the property, we should aspire a lot higher than that. We are managing treasured gifts from a loving Father!

A better comparison might be borrowing something from a good friend—his boat, car, expensive tools, etc. If he trusts us enough to let us use something of high value, then we probably want to make sure we return it in a condition that's as good as or better than when we borrowed it.

With stewardship, we are not only to manage resources *for* the owner, but also manage in a way that reflects the owner's values and goals—his *vision*. Managers can't do their job well if they don't know what the owner wants. When I worked with clients, this was always a big issue. About 98%

of the time, the people came to us with pretty vague ideas about what they wanted to accomplish. So, a big part of my job was to ask them questions to help them uncover their vision—their larger dreams and long-term goals. Then I would use that insight to guide the advice I gave to them and the decisions I made on their behalf.

So then, what is God's vision for His resources? Well, it's difficult to capture in one chapter, let alone one book. We have to study the Bible in its entirety to discover His vision. But it's there, and a big part of our job as stewards is to continually seek to understand it.

One of the passages of Scripture that I would be sure to include as part of God's vision is the Great Commission. Matthew 28:19-20 says, "Therefore go and make disciples of all nations, baptizing them in the name of the Father and the Son and the Holy Spirit, teaching them to obey everything I have commanded you...."

Another clear statement of God's priorities on the earth comes earlier in Matthew, when Jesus was asked which commandment is the greatest. He replied, "'Love the Lord your God with all your heart, with all your soul, and with all your mind.' This is the first and greatest commandment. The second is like it: 'Love your neighbor as yourself.' All the law and the prophets depend on these two commandments" (Matthew 22:37-39).

There are other places where God's vision is laid out, and there may be other convictions you have based on a more specific calling God has placed on your life. There were times when Jesus praised extravagant acts of generosity—what some people considered wasteful. In other places, he told his followers to "Sell your possessions and give to the poor. Provide yourselves purses that do not wear out – a treasure in heaven that never decreases, where no thief approaches and no moth destroys. For where your treasure is, there your heart will be also" (Luke 12:33-34).

Once we are aware of His commandments and what He wants to accomplish in the world, that vision should consume us, and we should hold it in mind as we manage the Owner's resources—including our time, our energy, our opportunities, and definitely our money. Stewardship is about leveraging those things for maximum effect to help bring about God's vision.

How are you treating the possessions in your control? Are you using them to glorify God? I hesitate to get too nit-picky with this. God does want us to be alert and wise, but I don't believe He wants us to be so worried about every money decision that we can never relax or enjoy His blessings in our lives. The details of how each person carries out stewardship are really between him and God.

Does God care about which brand of toothpaste you buy, which car model you drive, or which movie you pay ten dollars to watch? Maybe. Some decisions are more black-and-white than others. Also, different people might have different convictions about what's right in those situations, and they should follow those convictions. I believe God is usually more concerned about whether we're seeking to please Him as we make those decisions and go about our business.

What difference does it make in everyday life knowing that God owns your house, your television, your bank account, your wife and children? That awareness should change your attitudes and your actions, shouldn't it? For one thing, it will probably make you more grateful for the blessings He has placed in your path.

There's a key question that every steward must ask himself: Is this decision moving me one step closer towards God's vision for me and my family, or one step away from God's vision for me and my family? Again, the question applies to all our stewardship choices, especially financial ones.

I know I have a long way to go in many areas of stewardship, but I have found that a clear understanding of God's ownership and my role as a steward is very helpful as I make choices and seek to live a life that's pleasing to Him.

Pleasing Him is, after all, the end goal for all of us, right? We want to hear Him say to us, "Well done, good and faithful slave! You have been faithful with a few things. I will put you in charge of many things. Enter into the joy of your master" (Matthew 25:23).

Chapter 5
Be an Advocate: Faithfulness

"Well done, good slave! Because you have been faithful in a very small matter, you will have authority over ten cities."   Luke 19:17

Now we move on to the "A" traits. If we are truly changed by the awareness that God is the Owner of all things and we are humble stewards of His resources, and if, because of His truth, we have been "transformed by the renewing of [our minds]" (Romans 12:2), then it should show in our character. Our lives should be different in significant ways.

I believe that noticeable change will show up in four qualities described in Scripture. In a sense, we will become advocates for these qualities by the way we live and what we teach our children. An advocate actively pleads or defends a cause that's important to him, and that description fits here. We are to advocate for these four Biblical qualities because they are important for a life of righteousness *and* because they are vital parts of God's instruction on money. Each of these should be part of what we teach our children.

First on the list is **faithfulness**. The key question here is, "Whom do you serve?" In Matthew 6:24, Jesus said, "No one can serve two masters, for either he will hate the one and love the other, or he will be devoted to the one and despise the other. You cannot serve God and money."

Faithfulness addresses your loyalty, your primary allegiance. It's what you decide when someone asks, "Whose side are you on? You have to choose." When a husband or wife has an affair, we say he or she has been "unfaithful," and that's a useful picture here because too many Christians are "serving" the almighty dollar more than they're serving the almighty God. And God is saying we can't serve both. Are we living our lives on this earth for the purpose of making disciples or making money? If our money and possessions are getting our best time and attention, then we've made our choice. To Him, it must be like we're cheating on our relationship with Him; we're trading something precious, lasting and beautiful—the very best that He wants for us—for things that, in comparison, are cheap trinkets. They might hold our attention for a little while, then we're off to something else. He wants us to be faithful to Him and His vision.

Another big question is, "Why are you doing what you are doing?" English religious leader John Wesley summed up his approach to stewardship in the famous quote, "Make all you can, save all you can, give all you can." Are you earning and saving all the money you can to improve your lifestyle and give your family members everything they could ever want, or are you making and saving all you can to give all you can to further the kingdom of God?

We all need money, but even more than that, we need to be faithful and obedient to God. And as my wife often says, our actions speak louder and more clearly than words. I know our kids would agree with that. No matter what we say is most important, our actions send a more powerful and convincing message. This is true in relationships, and it's true in our stewardship.

The book of James confirms this: "For just as the body

without the spirit is dead, so also faith without works is dead" (2:26). Suppose you died today and the people who knew you were asked, "Did his actions match his words?" What would they say? Does your faith have action?

I love the story about the town that was facing severe drought:

> The fields were parched and brown from lack of rain, and the crops lay wilting from thirst. People were anxious and irritable as they searched the sky for any sign of relief. Days turned into arid weeks. No rain came. The ministers of the local churches called for an hour of prayer on the town square the following Saturday. They requested that everyone bring on object of faith for inspiration. At high noon on the appointed Saturday, the townspeople turned out en masse, filling the square with anxious faces and hopeful hearts. The ministers were touched to see the variety of objects clutched in prayerful hands ... holy books, crosses, rosaries. When the hour ended, as if on magical command, a soft rain began to fall. Cheers swept the crowd as they held their treasured objects high in gratitude and praise. From the middle of the crowd one nine-year-old girl's faith seemed to overshadow all the others—she had brought an umbrella.

Like that little girl, faithfulness isn't just saying you believe something; it's acting on that belief. It's making plans based on God's promises. As it says in Hebrews 11:1, "Faith is being sure of what we hope for, being convinced of what we do not see." Do you place your faith in your abilities, or God's? Are you sure that God will do as He says? God is the only one who will never let us down. Will your faith move mountains or mole hills?

When it comes to money, we must demonstrate our faith in

Dad Cents

God, not in the money itself. He is the great Provider; money is simply a tool, an area of life in which we need to be faithful to Him. Like most people in the story, many of us tend to serve (or be faithful to) treasured objects (money) instead of serving Him and believing His promises. We need to bring our umbrellas!

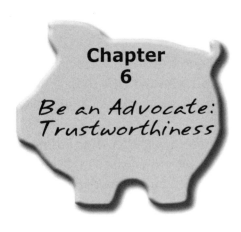

Chapter 6

Be an Advocate: Trustworthiness

"... they were unable to find any such damaging evidence, because he was trustworthy and guilty of no negligence or corruption." Daniel 6:4b

Has one of your children ever used something of yours and damaged it while he had it? Chances are, if that thing had any value at all, you talked to your child about being more careful. Then, as a good steward of God's resources, you probably made sure your child couldn't get to other valuable things and break them. He or she had to demonstrate more responsibility and earn back your trust, right?

That's also an example of our relationship with our heavenly Father. Being good stewards for Him is a testing ground, a preparation for eternity. We (and someday, our children) have to show ourselves **trustworthy**. Many things in life are more important than money—things that money cannot buy. But managing our money wisely and resisting the temptations that money brings demonstrate our trustworthiness to God.

The Bible makes it clear that how we manage the resources God has entrusted to us on earth will determine what He will place in our trust in Heaven. Luke 16:10-12 says, "The one who is faithful in a very little is also faithful in much, and the one who is dishonest in a very little is also dishonest in much. If then you haven't been trustworthy in handling worldly wealth, who will entrust you with the true riches? And if you haven't been trustworthy with someone else's property, who will give you your own?"

Our actions on earth will affect our eternity in Heaven! For me, that realization hit me powerfully. It helped me to reconsider how I am using God's resources—my own trustworthiness. I often find myself asking, "Is this use of resources moving me or someone else a step closer to God or a step further away from Him?" More times than I care to admit, I don't like my answer to that question, and I change my approach in that case.

Daniel provides a great example of trustworthiness. He was so upright and dependable at his job that the other administrators basically couldn't stand him (see Daniel 6). That's often how it is when trustworthy stewards are around people who are mostly living for themselves. Those people become much more self-conscious and uncomfortable with their own level of integrity. And that was the case with these men—they were so concerned that they tried to find any flaw they could use against Daniel to tear him down and ruin his reputation. But they couldn't "because he was trustworthy and guilty of no negligence or corruption" (Daniel 6:4).

Daniel was trustworthy in all his duties, and especially in his allegiance to God.

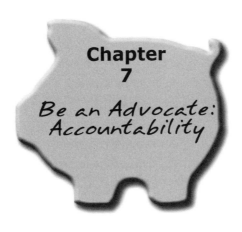

Chapter 7
Be an Advocate: Accountability

> "When [the king] returned after receiving the kingdom, he summoned these slaves to whom he had given the money. He wanted to know how much they had earned by trading." Luke 19:15

With money, just like in all of life, we are expected to be responsible stewards, and there will be a "day of judgment" regarding how we've done. We are **accountable**. This basic truth for our Christian lives is shown in this little parable:

One day God looked down on earth and saw all of the rascally conduct that was going on. He decided to send an angel to get a more accurate picture of the situation. After his visit, the angel returned and told God, "Yes, it's bad; 95% are misbehaving and 5% are not." God thought, "I want to get more data on this, just to make sure." So he called another angel and sent him to earth for the same task. The angel returned to God and said, "Yes, the earth is in decline. 95% are misbehaving and 5% are being good." God was not pleased, but He wanted His first move to be a positive one, so He e-mailed the 5% who were good, to encourage them to keep going.

Do you know what the e-mail said? Me neither! (I guess we weren't among the 5% who were good.)

As a Christian, you know about God's judgment. He is a God

of mercy and grace who has a plan to redeem even sinful people who place their trust in Him, but He also has expectations of His people. Remember Luke 12:48: "From everyone who has been given much, much will be required, and from the one who has been entrusted with much, even more will be asked." And in Romans 2, Paul writes, "He will reward each one according to his works: eternal life to those who by perseverance in good works seek glory and honor and immortality, but wrath and anger to those who live in selfish ambition and do not obey the truth but follow unrighteousness" (6-8).

Misbehaving or not, we must all give an account of our lives and our stewardship, like the slave in the parable who was held responsible for how he managed the king's money. To what standard are we held accountable?

The minimum standard is found in the king's statement to the third slave, who simply hid the money: "Why then didn't you put my money in the bank, so that when I returned I could have collected it with interest?" (Luke 19:23). We are to do something positive with the money God entrusts to us.

On the other hand, the maximum standard could be summarized in Jesus' statement to the rich young ruler in Luke 18: "Sell all that you have and give the money to the poor, and you will have treasure in heaven" (v. 22). As we'll see in another chapter, God does not look on us with favor when we try to hold on to all our money and material possessions when there is kingdom work to be done. In the parable of the rich fool, God demands everything—the man's very life! (Luke 12:20).

Now, looking at those examples, you might think, "That's a pretty wide standard—from 'Do something positive,' to 'Sell all you have and give to the poor.'" True, but we have to remember that Jesus' statement in each case addressed the issue that was keeping the man from devoting himself fully to God. Maybe one of those statements is appropriate for where you are, or maybe you're somewhere between the two.

The bigger issue is our faith. I believe He is most concerned about whether we're in right relationship with Him, and what issues may be standing in the way of us becoming more fully devoted followers of Christ. It's our job to acknowledge that He is the owner and we are stewards who are accountable to Him.

And we are accountable only for the amount that we have. Even if I could give every penny of my income to His work, I'm still limited by how much I earn. Some people will always give more than I do, and some people less, because of what God has chosen to give each of us. So none of us should beat ourselves up or feel inadequate as stewards because of what we can or cannot do in comparison to others. God has His reasons for giving us what we have. We are accountable to do our best with it, for His glory.

Chapter 8

Be an Advocate: Foresight

"Accumulate for yourselves treasures in heaven, where moth and rust do not destroy, and thieves do not break in and steal."   Matthew 6:20

As a boy, I was full of energy and had an almost unquenchable thirst for fun. I can remember one day walking into the kitchen without a care in the world. Much to my delight, right there on the table was a big blue balloon, calling out to me. It had to be punched! So I stepped back to get some momentum and gave it everything I could muster.

Pop! Crash! *Wow, what a loud noise for a balloon!* My mom rushed in to see if I had hurt myself. As things settled down, I soon realized that the "crash" didn't come from the balloon. There had been a drinking glass on the table, behind the balloon, which I hadn't seen.

As my mother helped me clean up the mess, I told her that I didn't know the glass was there; I didn't mean to break it. She understood, but used that opportunity to discuss why it's important to think about possible results before taking action. That was my first memorable lesson on the Biblical concept of **foresight**.

Trust me—being a male, I have many other examples of doing something without thinking of the possible outcomes. When

Dad Cents

I was ten, my cousin and I played a game at my grandparents' house. We put a board across one of the front steps with a rock strategically placed at one end. We'd jump on the other end and send the rock flying over the house. Great fun for a boy of that age, right? It was, until one time when my cousin jumped. He probably wishes the rock had broken a window, but instead it smashed into his forehead and within 15 seconds the front of his white shirt was covered in blood. He was fine, but he still has a noticeable scar.

Don't we all get frustrated with our children for similar reasons? We probably don't call it "foresight." We might say—especially to boys like I was—"You have to think about what you're doing." Or, "You need to slow down a little and look around you." Eventually, they learn that things aren't always as they appear to be, and there is often wisdom in taking a step back to survey a situation before taking decisive action. Ultimately, they may begin to ask questions like, "What are some of the possible outcomes if I do this ... or if I do *this* instead."

That's foresight: the ability to think ahead. We want our children to develop this skill, which will help lead them to make wiser choices, be able to delay gratification for a greater reward in the future, and other benefits.

Money provides many opportunities to talk about foresight with our children. Whenever a seven-year-old gets birthday money from Grandma, he wants to run down to the store and see what new toy he can buy. So his dad, applying foresight, might tell him, "You know, if you buy that today, it will take you longer to save up for that baseball glove you want." Then, a week later, when Junior is no longer interested in the toy and he sees something else he wants, his dad will probably say something like, "You know, if you hadn't bought that other toy with your birthday money, you'd have enough to get this."

Later in the book, we'll look at why it's important to start giving children opportunities to make decisions with a little bit of money, so they can learn more lessons from experience. Some children learn more effectively from experiencing the consequences of bad choices. But still, we can try to teach our children to have foresight in this area.

The world is full of adults who haven't learned foresight when it comes to money. They can't think beyond the next big-ticket item that calls out to them—or else they don't care what's beyond it—so they don't anticipate the debt they could get into or the other messes they may have to clean up because of poor spending decisions.

What better foresight could we have than to take to heart Jesus' words about sending treasure on ahead to heaven? In Matthew 6, he said, "Do not accumulate for yourselves treasures on earth, where moth and rust destroy and where thieves break in and steal. But accumulate for yourselves treasures in heaven, where moth and rust do not destroy, and thieves do not break in and steal. For where your treasure is, there your heart will be also" (19-21). We know heaven is our home and we are only in temporary dwellings. So, if we know what is going to happen, why don't we live like we have this knowledge?

Foresight takes time to learn, so we have to keep at it—and this is especially true for our children. But I do believe it will help them make better decisions about earthly matters and heavenly ones. By thinking ahead, the chances greatly increase that our money decisions, and our children's, will be more about glorifying God, less about the influence of advertising, and less about what kind of house, car, or clothing other people in the world believe we need to own.

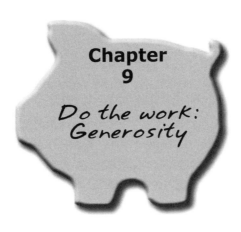

Chapter 9

Do the work: Generosity

"So it is with the one who stores up riches for himself, but is not rich toward God." Luke 12:21

Now that we have the key concepts and character traits laid out, it's time to put all that into action. This is where we find out if our good intentions and our faith really amount to anything. As it says in James 2, "What good is it, my brothers and sisters, if someone claims to have faith but does not have works?" (v. 14). So anything we claim to believe must be put into action, or it won't really make a difference.

James 1:22 says, "Do not merely listen to the word, and so deceive yourselves. Do what it says" (NIV). And 1 Chronicles 28:20 offers a similar exhortation: "Be strong and courageous, and do the work. Do not be afraid or discouraged, for the LORD God, my God, is with you" (NIV). All the principles we just looked at in relation to money won't impact our own lives and our children unless we live them out on a day-to-day basis, because our efforts to teach them will be meaningless unless we're demonstrating those virtues and actions in addition to talking about them. It has often been said that values are *caught* as much or even more than they are *taught*. We have to walk the *walk*, not just talk it. In this section, we'll look at five different actions the Bible suggests as ways to do that.

The first action that flows most naturally out of what we have described so far is **generosity**. If we fully understand God's *ownership* of everything and we are *faithful* to His calling on our lives regarding *stewardship*, and if we are *trustworthy*, have a high sense of *accountability*, and apply Godly *wisdom*, then I believe acts of generosity are the most logical next step for us. A clear understanding of what God has done for us should motivate us to help others and seek to bless others as we are able. Many times, generous giving is good stewardship.

One Saturday, Dan was preparing pancakes for his sons, five-year-old Kevin and Ryan, who was three. The boys began to argue over who would get the first pancake. Their dad saw the opportunity for a Biblical lesson. "If Jesus were sitting here, He would say, 'Let my brother have the first pancake, I can wait.'" Kevin turned to his younger brother and said, "Ryan, *you* be Jesus!"

Financial learning can begin at an early age—even young children are more perceptive than most people realize. Having children at ages 7, 5, and 4, I see this on a regular basis. Like Kevin and Ryan's dad, my wife and I attempt to convey the truths that Jesus talked about in His sermons and His parables. And, like this dad, sometimes we don't get the results we want. Selflessness and generosity don't come naturally to most of us.

In the Parable of the Rich Fool, Jesus gives us a good example of what we are *not* to do, and I think it's a fitting reminder for people in the 21st century. In response to a question about a dispute over an inheritance, Jesus tells a story about a man whose fields produced an abundance of crops—more than he had room to store. Clearly, the man's first thoughts are not toward generosity. He thinks it's time to enjoy life and take it easy, resting in the false security of his wealth. Jesus continues: "But God said to him, 'You fool! This very night your life will be demanded back from you, but who will get what you have prepared for yourself?' So it is with the one who stores up riches for himself, but is not rich toward God" (Luke 12:20-21).

Here's another illustration: A very wealthy man and his gardener died on the same day. The wealthy man had paid the gardener very poorly and had "paid" God (in giving to the Church) very poorly as well. The wealthy man hoarded all of his money and enjoyed most of the pleasures of the world. The gardener lived very shrewdly and gave sacrificially to God.

As they both approached the gates of heaven, they were greeted by St. Peter. After they signed in, Peter said he would be taking both men to their eternal homes in heaven. They approached an enormous mansion that amazed both men; it made the wealthy man's home on earth seem like servants' quarters. St. Peter told the gardener that this was his home.

The wealthy man thought to himself, *If this is his home, I can't wait to see my mansion*! St. Peter continued walking until he came to a dilapidated, one-room shack. Peter said, "This is your home in heaven!" The wealthy man couldn't believe it. "There must be some mistake!" St. Peter replied, "We did what we could with what you sent ahead!"

Imagine you are working in a foreign country and making a great wage, but you can't take any money or possessions home with you when you're done. The only money you can keep is what you send home. What would your dwelling look like in that country? Would you spend the equivalent of $2,000 per month on a house payment, or $500 per month on rent? Would you drive a Mercedes or Lexus, or ride public transportation? Would you live as meagerly as possible so you could send as much home as possible, or live a life of luxury and leave everything in the foreign country?

Dads, our home is in heaven! We need to be sending our treasure home. Jesus said, "But accumulate for yourselves treasures in heaven, where moth and rust do not destroy, and thieves do not break in and steal" (Matt. 6:20).

What would you do differently if Jesus were with you in person, watching you spend every penny? Would this influence your lifestyle decisions? If your job depended on how you spent your money, would you make any changes?

So, what does it mean to be "rich toward God"? How do we send our treasure home? Does it mean giving more to the church and other causes that we know God values? Maybe. That's definitely one way to give generously, although we know that God is more concerned about our hearts than the amount we give. Jesus said, "Where your treasure is, there your heart will be also" (Matt. 6:21). And in Luke 21, Jesus praises the widow's offering of two copper coins more than the great amounts that the rich were able to give, because she gave sacrificially (vv. 1-4).

We find another great way to be generous in Matthew chapter 25, where Jesus tells his disciples that whatever they do to help "the least of these," they are doing for Him (vv. 31-46). So generosity is also expressed in acts of kindness to the poor and suffering. That's another great way to be rich toward God.

First Timothy 6:17-19 says, "Command those who are rich in this world's goods not to be haughty or to set their hope on riches, which are uncertain, but on God who richly provides us with all things for our enjoyment. Tell them to do good, to be rich in good deeds, to be generous givers, sharing with others. In this way they will save up a treasure for themselves as a firm foundation for the future and so lay hold of what is truly life."

Ultimately, our generosity is motivated by our love for

Christ, as we discover in 1 John 3:17-18: "But whoever has the world's possessions and sees his fellow Christian in need and shuts off his compassion against him, how can the love of God reside in such a person? Little children, let us not love with word or with tongue but in deed and truth."

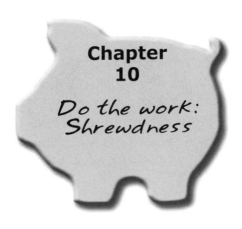

Chapter 10

Do the work: Shrewdness

"To impart shrewdness to the morally naive, and a discerning plan to the young person." Proverbs 1:4

In Luke chapter 16 we find a record of Jesus' telling of the parable of the clever steward, or the shrewd manager. It's a parable that has been confusing or even objectionable to some people. You may recall the story: A rich man fires his manager because he had wasted the master's resources. So the manager goes out and seemingly cuts deals with people who owe his master money. He reduces their debts so they will pay more quickly, and the rich man commends him "because he acted shrewdly." Jesus comments, "For the people of this world are more shrewd in dealing with their contemporaries than the people of light. And I tell you, make friends for yourselves by how you use worldly wealth, so that when it runs out you will be welcomed into the eternal homes" (vv. 8-9).

Now, I won't go into a detailed discussion here about every question that this parable raises. Is the manager being praised even though he appears to have cheated his master? What aspects of the manager's actions are being praised? And is the master completely without reproach, or could it be that he was charging the debtors an unfair amount of interest? The list of questions goes on, and I encourage you to do more study yourself.

Dad Cents

In the end, the point seems to be that this manager, in his desperation after being fired, took action to gain favor with those debtors in the event that they might be able to help him in at some point in the future. He used foresight! Though he had made mistakes in the past, he was resourceful in planning for his future, and that helped him regain the respect of his master.

In a similar way, Jesus wants us to use our money to influence people for eternal purposes—reaching out in love and kindness, and other acts that make our faith more contagious. We are to be shrewd in how we use His money for eternity.

Frankly, until recently I had never been fond of the word "shrewd." It always had negative connotations, like being "crafty" or "dealing with others in a clever underhanded way." But another definition is "showing or possessing intelligence, insight, and sound judgment, especially in business or politics [2]" as stated by the Encarta Dictionary.

A friend of mine, Duane Cantrell, former president of Payless ShoeSource, told me, "Know your vision, but keep the present in focus." Like the shrewd man, we should be thinking of the future, but we can't be so preoccupied with looking off in the distance that we stumble over something right in front of us. Shrewd stewards have that long-term vision, but they also keep the present in focus and act wisely and decisively in the situation before them. A shrewd dad is mindful of God's bigger purpose for him and his family, but he also makes the most of the daily opportunities to bond with and invest in his children. So, part of being shrewd is living intentionally.

I have always had a knack for finding the lowest price on something. I like to think I'm practicing shrewdness, although some friends have made fun of my "deal-finding efforts." I still take pride in that, although it's getting much more difficult when I have my three beautiful daughters surrounding me.

Sometimes my good intentions go by the wayside when we're in the grocery store and they give me those irresistible smiles and say a sweet "Please, Daddy?" There has been talk of banning me from unsupervised trips to the store with them.

As you know, people often marry someone who is their opposite in many ways. When I married my wife, one of us was much more of a spender, and the other was a saver. I'll let you guess which was which, but let's just say that we have both changed!

My wife is awesome—and shrewd! She has adopted a policy to spend no more than $5 on any piece of clothing for our daughters. That may have to change in a few years, but she is demonstrating willpower and a commitment to the goal. Being shrewd takes effort! We all know how easy is it to go to the store and come home with five things (or twenty things) that weren't on the list. In our home, we are very familiar with every outlet mall within 500 miles. We know when most of the stores have their seasonal clearance sales. I know which pizza places will take coupons from their competitors. For us, that's making the most of the opportunities in front of us.

Another part of being shrewd is making good judgments. Entire books are written on how to make good decisions, so I won't try to tackle the whole subject. But the basics include knowing our options. Often, people don't slow down long enough to look over all their options before making a money decision, but doing so can be a tremendous advantage.

For example, one judgment call we have made is about the brand of shoes we buy for our daughters. After trying a variety of brand-name and non-brand-name models, we decided to start buying the brand name shoes. We find them on clearance or at the outlet mall, so the price isn't that much higher, and we find that they last long enough to be able to pass them down from one girl to the next, so it's really the best option. You may take a different approach, and for good reasons, but I hope you take the time and trouble to explore your options a bit and learn from experience.

I hope every man reading this book will take these ideas, pray and listen for how God directs him in specific ways. We could all be more shrewd, and my prayer is that God will lead each of us into habits that glorify Him.

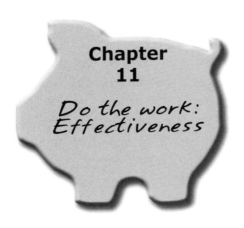

Chapter 11

Do the work: Effectiveness

"The prayer of a righteous person has great effectiveness."   James 5:16b

As Larry the Cable Guy says, "Git-r-done."

This may be the principle that best fits the "do the work" part of money stewardship. **Effectiveness** means completing something and achieving the desired results. It helps us discern whether we are being wise, shrewd, and faithful with God's money. What is the outcome?

A couple of years ago, I went through a very busy period in my life, and I had to have someone else manage my money. I just couldn't keep a consistent eye on my investments. For quite a few months, I didn't even get around to opening the statements for my account that arrived in the mail. Finally, I made an appointment with my investment representative.

What he revealed to me was surprising—and amazing! He had found a way to increase my $15,000 investment by 1100%! I was ecstatic. I had given him the money and had expected a decent return on it, but wow! Of course, my respect for that man grew tremendously. "Well done!" I told him. "You have been responsible with that relatively small amount of money, so here's another $150,000 to invest."

Dad Cents

By now you probably have figured out this story did not happen to me but is the Parable of the Ten Minas, from Luke 19, using a more modern situation. That parable, even without my version of it, provides some fitting examples of effectiveness. The first two servants were able to use their master's money to achieve the desired effect. They put the money to work exactly as instructed and successfully gained a good return—very good, in fact. The King tells the first two servants, "Well done!"

They were rewarded or not rewarded based on their effectiveness. The servant who earned 10 more was given charge of 10 cites, and the one who earned 5 more was given charge of 5 cities. The effectiveness of the first servant doubled that of the second servant. Jesus is instructing us to be productive with the money He allocates to us—as well as the time, talent, and opportunities he has put before us.

Effectiveness was also important to Paul. He spoke of being effective for God in 1 Corinthians 16:8-9: "But I will stay on at Ephesus until Pentecost, because a great door for *effective* work has opened to me ...." He knew that the opportunity in front of him really had potential to make a difference for the kingdom. James writes: "The prayer of a righteous person has great *effectiveness*" (5:16b). That man's prayers are lined up closely with God's will, and they bring about the desired results.

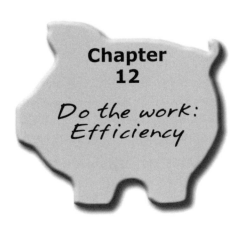

Chapter 12

Do the work: Efficiency

"Sir, your mina has made ten minas more."

Luke 19:16b

As I move to the next way we should be "doing the work" as stewards of God's money, I probably need to make a clarification. Many people confuse the words I've used in these two chapters—"effectiveness" and "efficiency"—and I understand how that could happen. In some settings, they are almost synonymous.

For our purposes here, I want to distinguish between the two. "Effectiveness," as I mentioned, is getting the desired results. The key is *completion*. With "efficiency," we're looking more at how the results were achieved. Was the best method used in order to reach the finish line? Usually there is an element of *time* involved, or sometimes we can look at how other resources played into the equation. If you look at a finished project and it's clear that something valuable was wasted in the process—like time, energy, opportunities, or money—then you probably have a good example of inefficiency.

Remember my fictional application of the parable in the last chapter that resulted in the $150,000 windfall? A few of you probably are asking, "But how long was the money invested?" Good question. That was my first thought. I calculated a few returns based on differing times. If the man of noble birth in the parable was gone for 5 years, the first servant's return would be 61.54% per year. If he were gone 10 years, 27.1%; 20 years, 12.74%; and 30 years, 8.32%. A time frame is not given, but I'm going to assume it's ten years or less—probably much less. His words and rewards to the faithful stewards seem to indicate they had done something really outstanding, and the 20- and 30-year returns, while nothing to sneeze at, are pretty close to what one would expect from an investment during normal economic times. I believe these guys did it in a much shorter time span.

Whatever the case, you see that efficiency has the time component. Efficiency actually depends on effectiveness as well. Here's another example of the relationship between the two: At a transmission repair shop, two different mechanics are working on the same problem on two separate cars. One mechanic repairs the transmission in thirty minutes, but the transmission does not work. He gets high grades for the time aspect of efficiency, but he failed because he was ineffective at attaining the desired result. The second mechanic repairs the transmission and it works well, but he takes two weeks to get it done. We would say that mechanic is very effective, but also very inefficient.

As we teach our children about money, we want them to become **efficient**—able to get things done in a timely manner—and **effective**.

During my financial consulting years, I heard another great example of efficiency or lack thereof. Imagine you are in a boat that is traveling up a river. The boat keeps a steady speed of 10 knots, and after an hour you look around and you haven't moved relative to the riverbank. What is your problem? The current is counteracting your engine. The gauges say you are doing something you are not. You have wasted an hour of time, and quite a bit of gas. What is your efficiency?

Take a look at your pay stub. Do you receive the full amount of your check? Of course not! What is counteracting or placing drag on your pay? Income tax, social security tax, Medicare tax and health insurance are some of the common drags. What about your investments? You pay management fees for your mutual funds, 12b-1 fees, mortality charges, morbidity charges, IRA fees and trade charges. The increasing prices of gas, stamps and milk are putting a drag on your money. Your bank account isn't growing as quickly as it could be.

Most of the individuals and families that I've worked with knew they were grossly inefficient. I would challenge you to take a look at how you spend and have spent your money—God's money. Have you been both effective and efficient? What would your children learn based on what they see in your spending patterns?

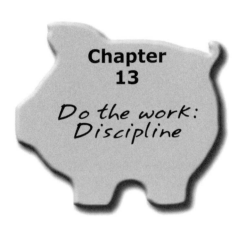

Chapter 13

Do the work: Discipline

"... some among you are living an undisciplined life, not doing their own work but meddling in the work of others." 2 Thess. 3:11

Discipline is another key to stewardship that shows up in our day-to-day actions. It helps to give direction and purpose to whatever good ideas or intentions we may have.

Here's a much better source on the topic. In 1 Corinthians chapter 9, Paul provides a great word picture for discipline:

"Do you not know that those who run in a race all run, but only one receives the prize? Run in such a way that you may win. Everyone who competes in the games exercises self-control in all things. They then do it to receive a perishable wreath, but we an imperishable. Therefore I run in such a way, as not without aim; I box in such a way, as not beating the air; but I *discipline* my body and make it my slave, so that, after I have preached to others, I myself will not be disqualified" (24-27, emphasis added).

During my athletic exploits earlier in life, I entertained thoughts that someday I might pursue sports as a career. Baseball was the sport where I experienced the most success. Our high school team was incredibly talented, and the coach was known for taking guys who lacked focus and self-discipline and turning them into a great team. Many of the individual players went on to get college scholarships and some were major league draft choices.

We had some great players, but one guy really stands out in my memory. He was a great pitcher and hitter. He had a 99-mph fastball, and I vividly remember seeing him hit a home run that must have traveled nearly 500 feet. (I was on the opposing team that night, and I had a perfect view of it from center field.)

Later, I joined the team he played for, but right after that he was drafted by the Detroit Tigers and left. The sad part of the story is that he only lasted a few years in the big leagues. He struggled with the temptations that many young men with money face. He's a good example of talent and potential that is wasted because of a lack of discipline.

How do you define discipline? Most often, discipline means resisting the temptation of quick pleasure in favor of a greater good. It's delaying gratification, working hard and possibly enduring pain and difficulty to attain a higher goal. That's what Paul is describing in his physical training word pictures, and what my former baseball teammate couldn't do. In the parable I have mentioned several times, the two good stewards put their master's money to work. I take that to mean that they decided on a plan and carried it out with discipline.

The applications for your children and their understanding of money should be obvious. When they start managing money, they'll be tempted to take those first nickels and dimes and head down to the store for as much candy and toys as they can get. In time, with your help, they'll learn that by saving their money and waiting a few weeks, months, or even years, they can afford things that may be much better and longer lasting.

At the start, their discipline or lack of discipline will affect their decisions about toys and candy, but through the years the stakes will only get higher. By the time they leave your home, they'll be making decisions involving money that could have life-changing ramifications.

It's vital that we train our children to have discipline. It will benefit them in their stewardship of money, but also in many other areas of life. For most children, living by God's directions while at home under Mom's and Dad's watchful eyes is much easier than continuing to follow those directions after they leave home, when no one is watching. That's when their discipline will really be put to the test. Our best course of action is to prepare them for that day now. Help them learn about the benefits of discipline and how they will be blessed when they follow God's desires for their daily lives.

Chapter 14

Learn the Secret of Contentment

"I have learned to be content whatever the circumstances. I know what it is to be in need, and I know what it is to have plenty. I have learned the secret of being content in any and every situation, whether well fed or hungry, whether living in plenty or in want. I can do everything through him who gives me strength."
Philippians 4:10b-13 NIV

How long do Christmas gifts hold the kids' interest around your house? If your kids are anything like mine, they go crazy with excitement for about a day after they open their presents. Then those new toys—the items they wanted so badly just a few days earlier—are thrown aside or stored in closets and boxes with all their other toys.

Our world is constantly inventing new things for our children to want, making them discontent with what they have. Okay, I confess. It happens with me sometimes too. Occasionally I get excited about some new tool or electronics gadget, and it isn't long before the shine has faded, maybe I discover its limitations, and it quickly becomes just another "thing" in the garage or basement.

In our world, we are bombarded with advertisements designed to make us discontent with what we have. If they can get us to believe that something better is always out there—

something that will make our lives easier, more fulfilling, and give us a sense of being accepted and happy—then the battle is mostly over. We're well on our way to spending our money on that "new and improved" product.

Maybe that's why there's a "secret" to **contentment**. Contentment is so rare today, and it seems clear that it's always been that way. Can't you just imagine the thought process of the third steward in the parable we've been looking at? "But John got five talents and Thomas got two! He only gave me one. That is not fair! What am I going to do with one? I might as well keep this one somewhere safe. Where should I keep it? What about the bank? No, they will have record of this money. What about in my sock drawer? No, my wife might find it! I know, I'll bury it in the back yard so no one will know where it is or that I have it."

Jesus is clear that each steward was given an amount to match his ability. Most of us think we are more responsible than we are—we can handle the temptations that come with wealth, or at least we're certainly willing to try. But this parable seems to say that God entrusts us only with as much as we're able to steward responsibly. So, not everyone is able to handle millions of dollars or a large business. If God gives everyone an amount suited to his ability and you're unhappy with what you have, does that mean you're questioning God? You are supposing that you know better than God. Part of being content involves knowing our own abilities and trusting that God knows what is best and He will provide for us.

In 1 Timothy chapter 6, Paul tells us that some false teachers at that time were using religion to get rich. Their "godliness [was] a way of making a profit." But Paul counters with this statement: "Now godliness combined with contentment brings great profit. For we have brought nothing into this world and so we cannot take a single thing out either. But if we have food and shelter, we will be satisfied with that" (vv. 6-8). Contentment is the added ingredient that makes the difference.

Hebrews 13:5 says, "Your conduct must be free from the love of money and you must be content with what you have, for He has said, 'I will never leave you and I will never abandon you.'"

Paul makes a similar statement in Philippians 4:12: "I know what it is to be in need, and I know what it is to have plenty. I have learned the secret of being content in any and every situation, whether well fed or hungry, whether living in plenty or in want" (NIV).

How many times have you read that verse and wondered, "What is the secret of being content?" Until recently, I hadn't even pondered the idea of a secret being associated with contentment.

When I researched other people's ideas on the secret of contentment, I found many different answers. Some fell into the "do not do this" category: do not covet, be lazy, love money, be selfish, be lustful, be greedy, etc. Other suggestions had positive actions we should do: give money, deny yourself, have the right timing, be patient, etc. Somehow, none of those seemed convincing. They all seemed to lead me to more questions, or maybe they didn't provide me with the feeling that I had discovered something that could be called a "secret."

Then I turned back to Philippians chapter 4 again and found a very familiar verse that I had never really read in its context before. I memorized the verse years ago, but I never read it as the completion of Paul's statement about the secret of being content. As you probably know, verse 13 says, "I can do everything through [Christ] who gives me strength." Of course! Contentment through Christ! The only way we can truly experience contentment is to depend on Jesus.

I compare that statement with John 14:6, where Jesus

says, "I am the way, and the truth, and the life. No one comes to the Father except through me." Just like the only way to heaven is through Christ, the only way to gain contentment is also through Jesus. That's the feature of Christianity that sets it apart from every other world religion.

When it comes to money, contentment is probably the biggest challenge for people—Christians included. Discontentment is the root of many bad decisions, and one common result is a mountain of debt. The way I look at it, piling up debt is like telling God that He isn't big enough to supply our needs. That probably isn't what Christians are thinking when they go into debt, but that's the attitude about God that their actions demonstrate.

Now, I'm not saying I do not have any debt or never have had debt. I have! For the first time in almost 13 years, my wife and I do not have any debt on our vehicles. As I look back at the decisions we made when we have taken on debt, I'm convinced that, in each decision, we could have done without those things for which we borrowed money—or at least we could have delayed getting them. So, I am guilty in some of these same areas, and I'm still learning and growing. God has revealed more and more to me, even during the process of studying His Word as I wrote this book.

I entertained the idea of including contentment in the "Discover" section. Ideally, this is a concept that we and our children will have in place already as we carry out the other principles and actions of good stewardship. If we're content, then it's much easier to grasp and apply the other ideas. But I soon realized that this is such a huge challenge in today's world, and contentment may be better seen as the completion of the process. It's the reward, the desired result of applying the earlier concepts. And it isn't that easy to attain, especially for children. Working through the other aspects of stewardship prepares us to more fully appreciate the value of contentment.

Contentment is one of the best traits we can teach our children, but it's also one of the most difficult. Content children, once on their own, will have a greater chance of living on a budget, not trying to keep up with the Joneses, giving to the church, having considerably less debt, having a happier marriage and being less costly to society.

Economists Andrew Clark and Andrew Oswald of Warwick University suggest that contentment is less costly than discontentment. Though we know money cannot buy happiness, these researchers came up with a way to measure, in financial terms, how different life events influence a person's well-being. For example, marital bliss is comparable to the added happiness of having an extra $110,000 per year in income, but losing a spouse brings a degree of unhappiness that would take an extra $210,000 per year to offset. A major health challenge results in a loss of happiness that scored a staggering $770,000 per year to overcome![3] But the most eye-opening finding for me is that a South African making $200 per year was found to be just as happy and fulfilled as an American making $70,000 per year![4] Be content with where you are!

A good place to start for all dads and children is gratitude. When we can appreciate the large and small blessings in our lives, we're much more likely to be content. An "attitude of gratitude" can radically alter how we go through life. As the saying goes, "Success is getting what you want. Happiness is wanting what you get."

Dads, we're sitting on a miracle right now. God has given us and our children everything we need to live rewarding and fulfilling lives. Maybe it's time we really understood what that well-known verse really means in the 23rd Psalm: "The LORD is my shepherd, I shall not be in want" (v. 1, NIV).

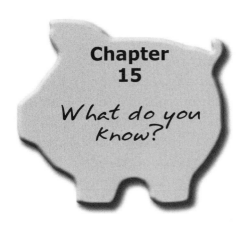

Chapter 15

What do you know?

"Of what use is money in the hand of a fool, since he has no intention of acquiring wisdom?"   Proverbs 17:16

A young man traveling in a far country was nearing the end of that day's journey, and he knew he needed to stop to rest soon. He was also very thirsty. He came upon a white-haired old man sitting by the side of the road. The young man asked where he could find water to drink, and the old man assured him that, by staying on the path, he would soon come to a small stream, but it would be after dark before he reached it.

Then the old man added a somewhat puzzling comment: if the traveler would pick up a handful of pebbles from the stream bed, he would be both glad and sad. The young man thanked the old man and continued down the path.

Sure enough, even though it was quite dark, he found the stream and took a drink. The comment about the pebbles seemed silly, but out of curiosity he picked up a handful and put them in his pocket. He continued a short distance and found a good place to sleep.

In the morning, the young man remembered the pebbles. He brought them out of his pocket and looked at them in amazement. Sure enough, he simultaneously felt great sorrow and great happiness, for they were not just pebbles, but beautiful, sparkling jewels. He rushed back to the stream and searched frantically for more, but the opportunity was gone. All he saw were ordinary pebbles. Just like the old man said, he was happy that he had picked up the pebbles that he had, but also sad that he didn't pick up many more.

I like that story because it captures what we all experience at various points in our lives: if we could go back with the knowledge we have now and change some things in the past, we could work some situations to our advantage. I can think of several things I would do differently—mistakes I made or opportunities I didn't take full advantage of. They encompass money and material possessions, relationships, my faith journey and many other areas of life.

We can't change the past, but we can use the valuable knowledge we've gained through study or life experiences for our benefit and for our children. We can spare them some of the trial-and-error process we went through—and some costly mistakes. With help from this book and your own knowledge and experiences, you will be able to teach your children and help them avoid many common mistakes. You will empower them to be comfortable with money and godly stewardship, even in this increasingly complex information society.

What do you know?

The following quiz will give you a general idea of your "financial IQ." You can also take this on the website, www.dadcents.com, where it will be automatically scored.

1. By law there is a minimum liability limit on your car insurance.   True | False
2. If your golf clubs are stolen from your car, your car insurance covers the loss. True | False

What do you Know?

3. An umbrella liability policy protects for damages over and above your car and house insurance.   True | False
4. If your disability insurance is tax deductible, your benefit, if disabled, would be tax-free to you.   True | False
5. If you are disabled and have a group policy, your benefit could be lowered if you receive Social Security Disability Insurance.   True | False
6. If you leave your place of employment, COBRA will allow you to continue your health insurance indefinitely. True | False
7. Social Security is a good retirement plan. True | False
8. If you have a will, your family members will not have to deal with going to probate court. True | False
9. Term life insurance is intended to last forever. True | False
10. The death benefit of life insurance is tax-free. True | False
11. Interest received on savings accounts is tax-free. True | False
12. Certificates of Deposit are very risky.   True | False
13. Tax deferred and tax deductible is the same. True | False
14. Interest on your home mortgage is tax-deferred. True | False
15. Money you place in your 401k is tax-deferred. True | False
16. Roth IRAs are tax-free if the money is withdrawn after 59½.   True | False
17. Money in an IRA is very liquid.   True | False
18. The tax penalty for withdrawing money from an IRA before 59 ½ is 15%. True | False

19. If you own a bond you are acting as a lender to the issuing institution. True | False
20. If you own stock in a company you own a part of that company. True | False

If you took the quiz manually, the answer key is in the back of the book. How did you score? Here is the score guide:

1-5 correct – You need a lot of education.

6-10 correct – You need more education.

11-14 correct – You are in pretty good shape.

15-19 correct – You are in great shape.

20 correct – You must be an accountant or financial consultant.

How did you do on the financial IQ test? I hope it gave you a better picture of where you stand, and I hope it provided some motivation to keep learning and growing in your financial prowess.

What Do You Need to Know?

Jeff Foxworthy's TV game show is called "Are You Smarter than a 5th Grader?" I watch sometimes to see if Fox can find any adults who really are smarter than a 5th grader, and I've yet to see any contestants prove that they are. But is that an accurate picture? Are the adults really not as smart, or could it be that they've simply forgotten the needed information? I think that, in most cases, it's the latter. They haven't bothered to remember those answers because they haven't needed that information for many years.

As you've probably seen, many people take that approach in various other areas of life. They study and remember what they really need to know. And I've seen that, very often, the financial world is an area where people have let their education slide. I suppose that's one of many reasons why financial companies continue to make money and working families continue to accumulate debt.

Recently, in a span of about six months, I had the opportunity to speak to men's groups at six local churches—a total of about 400 men. On each occasion, I asked them, "How many of you are still using the financial education that you received from your father?" Any guesses on how many guys raised their hands—total? Four!

Not only do we have *little* financial education from generation to generation, but *misinformation* is a big problem also. During my years as a financial consultant, when I met with clients to discuss their retirement goals, I regularly asked this question: "Would you rather have 5 million dollars that is 100% taxable at retirement, or 4 million dollars that is tax-free at retirement?" Amazingly, every person I asked told me they would rather have the tax-free money. But, when we would look at their personal retirement savings, they were going to have all or most of their money subject to income tax. Why? They didn't know that a tax-free option was available.

So, the big lesson is to learn as much as you can about your situation. When was the last review you had with your property and casualty agent? Have you ever visited the benefits person at your company? Have you met with an attorney for a will and power of attorney for medical and financial decisions? Have you ever met with your banker to make sure you have the best account for your family?

During the time I spent in the world of financial consulting, I found out why that profession was created. There's a never-ending stream of information to keep up with, old and new, and individuals can spend their days studying that information and be a help to others. As you might expect, I'm in favor of utilizing the services of a financial consultant. In most cases, he or she will have knowledge and expertise that you don't have.

As a brief aside, if you do use a consultant, make sure to interview him or her and be willing to ask some potentially touchy questions, such as:

1. Does he have spiritual convictions? (It's good if he does, but that doesn't mean he will always give you good advice!)
2. Can he *prove or verify* what he is suggesting to you, or is he suggesting what he *thinks* is the best?
3. Does he charge a fee? If the person you meet with charges a fee for his "advice" and wants to sell you the products in his plan, I'd advise you to run. Planners who charge a fee are not unbiased! I know honorable consultants who do not charge fees.
4. Is he tied to or obligated to only one company, or can he sell with multiple companies?

Now, back to my question that started this section: *What do you need to know?* The answer is, *As much as you feasibly can!* In order to be shrewd, you must have knowledge. At the same time, you don't want to become obsessed with financial information and strategies so that the pursuit of money becomes your master.

Remember, you are caring for your Master's possessions, and your focus must remain on His vision for your stewardship. Don't be afraid to ask for help if you need it—from friends, relatives, or someone in the financial field. Make sure to get several opinions before you make a decision.

Modeling

Do you remember when former NBA star Charles Barkley said, "I am not a role model"? Other professional athletes and celebrities have made similar statements. I can understand that they don't want to have to watch their behavior every minute of every day; they probably want to be able to enjoy life without that added pressure.

I touched on this topic in the very first chapter, and it's worth a brief mention again here. No matter what they or any of us might say, we are models. All of us create impressions on those around us by the way we live. We can only control what we do, not what anyone else thinks! And if we're responsible, we'll realize that people are watching us, and we'll try to be reliable models of good character.

Jesus was a great teacher, but He was also our ultimate model. In addition to reading what He said, we can also watch how He conducted Himself and how He dealt with people in the Gospels. He gave us a model life and a model prayer. What kind of a model are you?

Our oldest daughter grumbles under her breath when she gets frustrated. (I can't imagine whom she's copying.) I can also see ways in which my youngest daughter picks up on my behavior. All three of my girls love to play "monster," and of course I'm the monster. When I growl at them and chase them around our house, they run away from me, screaming with delight ... except for my youngest—she growls back!

Often, examples of modeling are cute, especially when children are young. But in many areas of life, our children's need for *reliable* models is very important. They need to see what a strong marriage is like; they need to see how to resolve conflict in a healthy way; they need to watch us do the routines of life with dignity, patience, and responsibility.

Stewardship of finances is one of those important areas where modeling is needed. It's crucial! The previous chapters highlight some of those virtues that you need to be modeling for your children. If your children do not see you tithing, why would they tithe? If they don't see you shopping for sales, how will they learn? If they never hear you talking about waiting a few months to get something you want, why would they ever save their money to buy something instead of going into debt? They will replicate what they see.

In the following chapters, I'll provide you with some key areas to focus on for children of different ages, with some practical suggestions to try. Many of my suggestions basically boil down to modeling character and virtues. Modeling is a powerful way in which you are already influencing and teaching your children. The challenge is to be intentional about what you're modeling and provide your children with a foundation built on Christ. And in the process, you'll build a stronger relationship with God yourself.

Imprinting

"Wow! Four dollars for a gallon of milk!" exclaimed Chad. He and his daughter Emily were at the convenience store getting milk. Chad's wife had called to ask him to get some milk while he was out, and the grocery store was out of the way. As Chad reached into the refrigerated case, he said to his daughter, "Emily, they charge a lot more for milk here than they do at the grocery store." He explained to her that sometimes convenience is a bigger factor than at other times, and people are willing to pay more for items.

Chad is trying to be intentional in his efforts to teach Emily about finances. Although she is only six, he has started to feed her mind with small ideas to begin molding her decision making process. You might say he's trying to use "imprinting" to plant seeds of good stewardship.

In case you aren't familiar with that term, it's typically talked about in marketing efforts. Every time someone is exposed to a particular brand name or logo, that message is burned into his mind. Assuming the experience is positive, the person is then more likely to look for that brand name or logo when he is looking for products that company sells.

Another example comes from Team Baby Entertainment, who has developed videos for small children that introduce the child to the parent's favorite pro or college sports team. You can look them up online.

"The goal of Team Baby Entertainment is to allow parents, grandparents, alumni and friends to share their love, loyalty and passion for their favorite teams with their children" says Greg Scheinman, Founder and CEO of Team Baby Entertainment. "Our product is an informative, entertaining and educational way to introduce a child to the university and/or team you root for."

The company realizes that early impressions can be the most powerful and long-lasting, and that infants and toddlers, even though they are just learning to walk and talk, have tremendous buying power. If they start liking Daddy's team colors, then Daddy will spend money to make sure they get to wear those colors.

Here is an incredible example: Dr. Tom Robinson and other researchers at Stanford University studied 63 kids in California. They used 5 pairs of identical food, except one item was in a McDonald's wrapper and the other in an unbranded package. The kids where then asked which one tasted better. As you might expect, the McDonald's wrapper made everything taste better to the kids.

The researchers came to this conclusion: "Branding of foods and beverages influences young children's taste perceptions. The findings are consistent with recommendations to regulate marketing to young children and also suggest that branding may be a useful strategy for improving young children's eating behaviors."[5]

You can see why this idea has become a bit controversial,

and it makes me wonder about all the imprinting that my children have received from different sources—some good and some bad. As parents, we must be vigilantly about the messages our children are taking in. We can't just give the world free access to the minds of our children.

Dad, what are you doing to counteract these influences? What are you doing to be intentional about teaching your children? I have no problem with videos for kids, but are they watching the videos for mindless entertainment, or do the videos also teach important (and even Biblical) truths?

Imprinting does work. The big question is, *Are you using it to intentionally plant seeds of faithfulness and Godly stewardship in your children—like Chad is doing—or are you letting your children be influenced by whatever messages happen to come along?* We must be shrewd and use every opportunity we have to lead our children closer to Christ and His will for our lives. And talking about financial ideas and concepts can begin at an early age.

Key Actions –

1. Increase your financial knowledge. Try to read one financial book each year. See www.dadcents.com for recommendations.
2. Consider meeting with a financial consultant, who can equip you to make good decisions and will not tell you what to do.
3. Be a model to your kids. Model Jesus.
4. Understand and use imprinting for positive ends. Be aware of vulnerabilities your children might have to messages in the world.

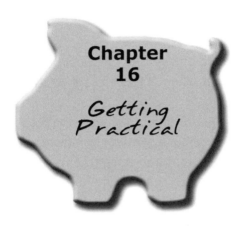

Chapter 16

Getting Practical

> "The kingdom of heaven is like a treasure, hidden in a field, that a person found and hid. Then because of joy he went and sold all that he had and bought that field." Matthew 13:44

Now we enter the part of the book that I believe might be the most helpful for you. Very soon, I'll provide you with practical ideas and actions to consider using with your children at their stage of life. In each chapter, I'll discuss some money ideas and issues that are appropriate for you to address with them during that stage. We'll get there all in good time.

But if you're one of those readers who likes to skip ahead to what interests you most—you want immediate help with your specific children—and you've landed here, then I understand and that's fine. But I do hope you'll go back and read the previous "D.A.D.S." section, either now or later. (They're really short chapters.) This part of the book will make more sense and should make more of a difference for you if you read it after having grasped—and, I hope, internalized—those principles and habits.

As much as I would like everyone to get this book and begin teaching their children money concepts at age three, I realize that won't be possible for everyone. Still, the steps I have laid out will be easier to utilize if you begin when your children are very young. That's when they're more likely to listen to you better, right?

If your children are older, the first few chapters that follow can be covered very quickly and you can catch up. Just make sure you make appropriate adjustments for your children's ages. And if your older children have already acquired a few bad habits, or have bought into ideas about money that contradict God's word, I believe the ideas you'll find, if implemented properly, can be used to retrain them and instill positive money habits.

Whatever ages your children are today, you can begin to teach them using this guide. Start at the beginning and build your foundation. Then, if you haven't yet, work your way through chapters 2-14 and begin to implement those principles and ideas as well.

I hope you understand that these principles will work best in a larger context of positive parenting habits. That includes being clear and consistent with your expectations; sticking to a punishment or rule you implement even when it isn't popular (and I know that's difficult); and exercising tough love with a child in order to get a message through to him.

Whether you're a dad with young kids, tweens, high schoolers, college-age kids, or even married children (with kids), you can implement the concepts in this book. Chances are, regardless of their age, your children still need to learn them. If they're older, you may just need to be a little more creative.

One more recommendation: it's important to understand your children's learning styles and use that information as you teach them. My wife and I have used a book called *The Way They Learn* by Cynthia Tobias to help us in this area with our daughters. I suggest you get your hands on that resource or another one which provides insight into learning styles.

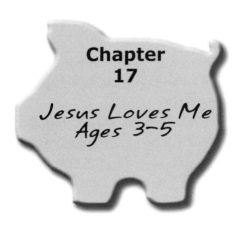

Chapter 17

Jesus Loves Me
Ages 3–5

"Fix these words of mine into your mind and being, and tie them as a reminder on your hands and let them be symbols on your forehead. Teach them to your children and speak of them as you sit in your house, as you walk along the road, as you lie down, and as you get up."   Deuteronomy 11:18-19

In the early years of your child's life, it's probably too much for him or her to start processing complex money principles. That doesn't mean you can't still model good habits and occasionally tell him what you're doing and why, but the main focus of your efforts should be on his faith in God. If he gets to his sixth birthday and understands that Jesus loves him and that God's Word is true, he'll be well on his way to thriving in many areas of life. His future stewardship of money is only one of many good reasons to give him that foundation of faith.

So, focusing on your child's faith is really the point of this chapter. It's simple, but not easy. Training your children begins at an early age, and financial training begins with teaching your children to have Jesus as their foundation. Child rearing and financial training fit hand in hand; the foundation is the same for both: Jesus!

Some days, my wife Val and I feel like our girls are getting the message. (Other days, not so much.) One Saturday not long ago, we left them with my sister and her family so Val and I could spend some errand time by ourselves. (Our girls love to play at their older cousins' house.)

Soon after we left, my sister called on our cell phone about a mini-drama involving our oldest daughter, Jerica. My sister said they were going to watch a movie, but the Jerica wasn't sure about that movie. You see, Jerica is always very particular about making sure she sees only movies that Mom and Dad approve of. Even after I discussed the movie with my sister and gave our approval, Jerica would not watch the "bad" movie. Her aunt and uncle tried to reassure her that we had approved the movie, but she had not heard it straight from her daddy, so she left and played elsewhere. She didn't want to disappoint us; she knew we preferred movies that show God's love. We were quite surprised when we heard about this, but we also were glad that she stuck with her convictions about what she believed was right.

King Solomon, whom we looked at earlier, is another good example of this principle. For much of his life, his foundation was on God and the rest of his decisions emanated from God's wisdom. That's what we all want for our children. By giving our children the correct foundation, they will begin to see the world as Jesus does.

I recommend starting with "Jesus loves me" and moving on to the fruit of the Spirit. (Love is included in that list too.) All children need to learn and practice these things. Seeing fruit in their lives will be a sign of a foundation on God as they grow and mature.

Teaching Jesus' Love

A farmer had some puppies for sale. He made a sign advertising the pups and nailed it to a post on the edge of his yard. As he was nailing the sign to the post, he felt a tug on his overalls. He looked down to see a little boy with a big grin and something in his hand. "Mister," he said, "I want to buy one of your puppies."

"Well," said the farmer, "these puppies come from fine parents and cost a good deal."

The boy dropped his head for a moment, then looked back at the farmer and said, "I've got thirty-nine cents. Is that enough to take a look?"

"Sure," said the farmer, and with that he whistled and called out, "Dolly! Here, Dolly." Out from the doghouse and down the ramp ran Dolly followed by four little balls of fur.

The little boy's eyes danced with delight. Then out from the doghouse peeked another little ball, this one noticeably smaller. Down the ramp it slid and began hobbling in a futile attempt to catch up with the others. The pup was clearly the runt of the litter. The little boy pressed his face to the fence and cried out, "I want that one!" as he pointed to the runt.

The farmer knelt down and said, "Son, you don't want that puppy. He will never be able to run and play with you the way you would like."

With that the boy reached down and slowly pulled up one leg of his trousers. In doing so he revealed a steel brace running down both sides of his leg that was attached to a specially made shoe. Looking up at the farmer, he said, "You see, sir, I don't run too well myself, and he will need someone who understands."

That's one example of how we can relate Jesus' love to young children—through stories. They'll hear the story and get a better understanding of what Jesus did when He came to earth to become one of us, to actually get dirty and walk with us. He understands.

"Jesus loves the little children, all the children of the world. Red and yellow, black and white, they are precious in His sight.

Jesus loves the little children of the world." My daughters love to sing that song. And I pray that they will come to know the depth of Jesus' love for them.

John 3:16-17 tells us the number one expression of God's love for us was that He "so loved the world that He gave His one and only Son, that whoever believes in Him shall not perish but have eternal life. For God did not send His Son into the world to condemn the world, but to save the world through Him." We must teach our children about love—the real kind of love that we see in the Bible.

One of the stories Jesus told to teach us about love is in Luke 15—the parable of the prodigal son. Even after the son's inconsiderate, short-sighted, foolish decisions and wild living, the father still showed him unconditional love. The story is a powerful demonstration of what love really is, and even young children can grasp that. As fathers, we need to make sure they have many opportunities to learn about real love.

My girls and I have a game we play. I will ask them, "How much does daddy love you?" Jerica will reply, "Thissss much!" and stretch out her arms as far as she possibly can. Jaley, our middle daughter, will stretch out her arms and say "Big much!"

Do your kids know how much you love them? They will see and experience love from you, their parents, and they'll learn to share that love with their siblings and others. Later in life, you will see that love expressed through their use of money. 1 John 3:17 tells us that if we have God's love, one way to express that love should be through generosity with our money and material possessions to others in need. Generous giving is a great way for your children to learn how to express love.

The Fruit of the Spirit

You probably know the list from Galatians 5:22-23: love,

joy, peace, patience, kindness, goodness, faithfulness, gentleness and self-control. They are the end result of a lot of work by the Holy Spirit! Have you noticed that when we become a child of God, we don't automatically start demonstrating all the fruits of the Spirit? Like me, you have always had self-control, right? I know some people with the self-control of a ten-year-old.

How long does a fruit tree take to bear fruit? One year, three years or five years? Standard apple trees are slow to start bearing fruit—usually about five to eight years. New varieties have been developed that can cut that time in half. Similar advances have been made for cherries, apricots, peaches, and so on.

But we also know that not all fruit trees bear fruit. Here's a description from Edmond L. Marrotte of the University of Connecticut Department of Plant Science:

> A fruit tree will normally begin to bear fruit after it has become old enough to blossom freely. Nevertheless, the health of the tree and its environment, its fruiting habits and the cultural practices used can influence its ability to produce fruit. Adequate pollination is also essential to fruit yield. If just one of these conditions is unfavorable, yields may be reduced or the tree may not bear any fruit at all. The grower can exercise some control over most of the factors contributing to fruit production.[6]

As you might have guessed, my point here is not just about apples, cherries and peaches. Read the description again, with the word "child" inserted for "fruit tree" and some other substitutions:

> A **child** will normally begin to bear fruit after [he] has become old enough to blossom freely [accept Jesus as

Savior]. Nevertheless, the health of the **child** and its environment [spiritual modeling by the parents and a home conducive to spiritual growth], its fruiting habits [quiet time and prayer] and the cultural practices used [spending time with other kids that sharpen spiritual senses instead of time with kids that dull spiritual senses] can influence its ability to produce fruit. Adequate pollination [allowing the Holy Spirit to work] is also essential to fruit yield. If just one of these conditions is unfavorable, yields may be reduced or the **child** may not bear any fruit at all. The grower [mom and dad] can exercise some control over most of the factors contributing to fruit production."

The "growing environment" is up to us as parents—especially fathers. We can create a godly environment where we model Jesus in a way that nurtures our children's spiritual growth and encourages habits of quiet times and prayer, so that the fruit of the Spirit will develop. (Those character qualities will also guide your children toward godly financial decisions.)

Allow me to make one more relevant point with help from the late Dave Simmons:

There are two contrasting perspectives that describe child-raising—should you function as a sculptor or a gardener? A sculptor sees a vision of the final figure in a block of stone and starts to hammer away, breaking, splintering, and cracking away the pieces that don't belong to his or her vision. A gardener takes the plant and creates the perfect environment for it so it can grow to its full potential.[7]

Clearly, "gardening" is the preferred approach. Dave further explained:

The picture I draw from this illustration is one of a

father doing whatever it takes to create the required conditions that allow a child to grow naturally to maturity.... [This] does not mean that you should knead, pound, and roll your child like dough .... You are not an architect and certainly not a sculptor to cut chunks of your child away until he suits you.[8]

Ideally, the process of training your children and helping them build a relationship with Christ should start at a very young age. But if your children are already school-age or in their teens, you still have time while they are in your house!

Application:

1. Read and discuss 1 Corinthians 13 with your children.
2. Tell them what love is and what love is not; read through the verses until they seem to have a grasp. You might think this is a little deep for young kids, but they will know what being kind means and what anger means.
3. Print from a computer or handwrite verses 1 Cor. 13:4-8 and post them on your refrigerator. That's a good place to remind family members about what love is, and you can refer to it there whenever needed.
4. Memorize the fruit of the Spirit with your children— Galatians 5:22-23. (There's a great kids' worship song that would be a big help.)
5. Go to our web site www.dadcents.com and utilize the spiritual fruit cut-outs. They are good visuals and your kids will enjoy coloring them.
6. pend regular time talking with your children about each of the fruit. Cycle through them, spending a

week on each fruit for the entire year. (You will be able to talk about each one approximately 9 times.) Have personal examples to share, and ask them to think of good and bad examples for each one.

7. Watch carefully for your children to demonstrate the fruit of the Spirit. When you see an example, point it out and affirm them.

8. Remember, each of your children has a different learning style. Make sure to give examples that will appeal to each style: auditory (hearing the information); visual (seeing the information); kinesthetic/tactile (touching and participation).

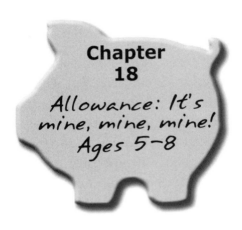

Chapter 18

Allowance: It's mine, mine, mine!
Ages 5–8

"Fathers, do not provoke your children to anger, but raise them up in the discipline and instruction of the Lord." Ephesians 6:4

"Daddy, can I go play in the front yard by myself?" Jerica asked.

"No!" I said.

"But Daddy, why?"

"Because," I said.

Again Jerica asked, "Daddy, can I go play in the front yard by myself?"

I repeated the same answer as before, and off she ran, crying in disappointment.

Have you ever experienced something like that with your kids? Of course you have. You probably have conversations similar to this just about every day. My girls keep asking and asking until I am exasperated. You'll notice, though, that Ephesians 6:4 says we are not to exasperate our children, not the other way around.

I eventually learned that "Because" or "Because I said so" are not good answers by themselves. I know sometimes we use those responses when we're tired and we don't have the energy to engage our children at the level of detail and with the patience that they need from us.

But the *Encarta Dictionary* defines the word "because" like this: "for the reason that follows."[9] But when we use it like I did, there was no reason following. That response doesn't tell a child anything about *why*. It doesn't teach her anything.

When Jerica asked about playing in the front yard, I should have said something like, "No, because I can't watch you to make sure you're safe." She would have still protested some, but at least she had something to think about—a "why" behind my answer—and she could deal with that and move on with life.

That's an example of what I believe Paul was writing about in Ephesians 6:4, when he told fathers to bring up their children in "discipline and instruction." That training and instruction is seeking and knowing God, but also practical everyday living. Money is a big part of that everyday instruction, and allowance can be a very practical avenue to instruct our children about God's directions for money.

Your house is a great testing ground for your children's future. The teaching and molding you give them while they are in your home—and the lessons they learn through experience, while the possible consequences are pretty small—will play a major role in their ability to be effective upon leaving your protection and guidance. Again, money is an important area where they need your instruction.

All children are different and all parents will have their own convictions about when to start an allowance, but many parents start sometime between ages 5 and 8. And of course, there are different approaches to how allowances are handled. I have convictions about all this, and I hope you'll at least consider my viewpoint.

The Purpose of Allowance

Imagine you are ready to play Monopoly with your children.

All the motels and hotels are out of the box, the board is set up and everyone has selected their playing piece. Now all you need is the money, but it's nowhere to be seen! How much fun would you have playing Monopoly without the money? You could try to explain how the game works, and you might even write down each player's bank balance on a score sheet. But it just wouldn't be the same, and I think your children would lose interest pretty quickly.

That's what it's like trying to explain how money works without using real money. How would you teach your kids to tithe, to save, to spend wisely, and how taxes work? How would you explain money to them?

The purpose of allowance is to give your children learning experiences with small amounts of money, so they're prepared for the later years, when higher dollar amounts come into play. Allowance is a tool that, when used wisely, will pave the way for your children to experience God's best throughout their life when it comes to money matters. Money in their hand gives you opportunities to teach them the attributes and characteristics that I mentioned earlier in the book—how to be shrewd, faithful, trustworthy, efficient, effective, accountable, generous, and so on. These can be taught without using money, but your children would do well to learn how they all relate to money.

Allowance will also give you teachable moments when you can introduce some key financial concepts. At 5 years old, my daughter knew the economic concept called **opportunity cost**. If you aren't familiar with that term, it refers to what must be given up—the other alternatives—whenever you make a decision. Any choice between two or more options has an opportunity cost. Jaley does not know the exact definition, but she knows how it works. She regularly gets to make a choice of dessert: ice cream, cookie or chocolate chips. Jaley understands that if she chooses ice cream, she will not get the other two. If she chooses ice cream, the opportunity cost (what she gives up) is the cookies and chocolate chips.

How does that relate to money? By giving her an allowance, even at 5 years old, she will be able to make similar choices with her money. When she gets her money and spends it the next time she's at the store, we'll tell her, "That's fine, but if you find something you want that's more expensive, you'll have to wait even longer to save for it." And a few days later, when she does see something else that she wants more, we'll simply say, "Sorry. You'll get another allowance next week."

That example brings up another economic term that is related to opportunity cost: **scarcity**. Scarcity describes the condition of limited resources, and unlimited wants and needs. Jaley only has a certain amount of money, but there are many toys she wants to buy—limited resources, but unlimited options.

God's definition of scarcity is quite different from the world's definition. I believe God would say we are living in a condition of His *unlimited resources*, but we should have *limited* wants and needs. He is more than enough for every need that we have. We should pursue Him and be content with what we have! What do we need to exist in this world? Food, water and shelter (clothing and a roof over head).

The world's prevailing view of scarcity says that we never have enough to keep up with our ever-increasing wants and needs. We are encouraged to keep attaining more and more, but we're forced to make difficult decisions based on limited resources.

While I certainly prefer God's approach to the topic, I believe we need to teach our children both definitions of scarcity. Looking at what I'm calling the "world's definition," our children need to learn to make good choices with the money they have, and they need to understand the dangers of not doing that. Many people in our culture do not let limited funds stop them from spending anyway; they simply charge it and go into debt rather than waiting to get what they want.

A very important part of teaching our children about scarcity is helping them learn to distinguish between wants and needs. That's a challenge even for most adults, so we would be wise to start talking about needs vs. wants with our children even at an early age. They can begin to develop a discerning eye in this area.

Once again, modeling is a key factor, because our children will compare what we say about wants and needs with what they *see us do*. Are we choosing what kind of clothes and shoes we wear based on needs or wants? Does that also apply to their toys? As they get older, they will be more aware of their peers and what their peers have, but their early awareness will come from you.

Earlier in the book, I mentioned the challenge I have whenever I take my daughters to the grocery store. For a while, they really worked me over: "Daddy, can I have one of those?" "Daddy, will you get this for me?" Eventually, my wife and I learned to utilize their allowances in these situations to help teach them about wants vs. needs. (Actually, it's an idea I learned recently, but my wife has been using it for quite a while.)

One Sunday, we were eating out after church—a "gourmet" lunch off the dollar menu at a fast-food restaurant. Our middle daughter Jaley asked, "Can I have some chocolate ice cream?" I immediately answered, "No," and she complained. When my wife and I had a minute to talk, she suggested a better answer for next time. And when Jaley asked again, we were ready for her. My wife told her that she could use her allowance to buy the ice cream. My daughter didn't have to think very long before she blurted out, "I guess I don't want any." She quickly figured out that the ice cream was a want and not a need, and the best part was that she made that decision herself, so there was no complaining.

Another important point is that Jaley made a different choice because we asked her to make a spending decision with *her own* money. This is worth another illustration:

Imagine what would happen if I took my daughters to a candy store and gave each of them two dollars to spend. As I hand them the money, I take one of two approaches. In the first scenario, I tell them, "Get what you want, and bring me back the change." How much do you suppose I'll get back? That's right, probably a few cents, because they will find ways to spend every bit of the money. But what if I told them, "Get what you want, and you can keep what's left." Now, odd as it may seem, they will probably spend less of the money. That's what happens when we make our kids feel like they're spending *their own money*.[10]

When our children feel like they are spending our money, they have no reason to think about their needs or place any limits on their wants. It's like a salesman with a huge expense account, or someone who wins a thousand-dollar shopping spree at the local hardware mega-store. He is much less likely to weigh his decisions or be thrifty.

But everything changes when it's *their* money—even if you have given it to them. When they know funds are limited, they start thinking about different uses for that money, and they make better decisions. Suddenly, baseball cards and ice cream don't seem nearly as important.

Now, this approach doesn't guarantee that they'll only buy necessities or save every penny for college; they'll still make bad decisions sometimes. But we hope they'll learn from their decisions—good and bad. And in the process, they will begin to understand scarcity, they'll be likely to spend time thinking about what they buy, and they'll consider some longer-term goals. And those things are important.

Even more importantly, we also need to teach our children that we serve a good God who will provide for their needs. In Psalm 37:25, David writes, "I have never seen a godly man abandoned, or his children forced to search for food." We can be confident that God is faithful to His promise. We don't know if He will provide us with much or little, but that is up to Him. Our responsibility is to be content with what He has given us to manage.

I would challenge you to try some practical and meaningful ways to teach your children about needs and wants, and how much they are blessed. For example, you might sponsor a needy child in another country and talk with your children regularly about how little that child has in comparison to them. Or, I know some families who have a rule that every time a child gets a new toy or outfit, they choose one of their other toys or outfits to give away to a child who has less, or an outreach to needy families. All around us there are opportunities to respond to people's needs and involve our children. If we make it a way of life, our kids will catch the message.

Were you familiar with the concepts of opportunity cost and scarcity? If you were, I am impressed. It could be that you knew the principles behind these concepts even if you haven't used those terms. If they are new to you, then you're in the normal range of most adults. Numerous authorities on financial matters will tell you that the economics understanding of the general public in our country leaves a lot to be desired. One publication of the Center for Entrepreneurship and Economic Education at the University of Missouri-St. Louis provides some details:

As adults, we are called upon to make economic decisions every day of our lives. However, this crucial life skill is virtually ignored in elementary and secondary education. For those who attend college, an economics course is often too little, too late. Those who forego college may never be educated in economics and, therefore, are seriously disadvantaged. According to a survey by the Gallup Organization, American adults and high school and college seniors know shockingly little about how the American economy works.

- While unemployment is the economic issue of most concern to Americans, three out of four do not know the unemployment rate.
- Seven out of ten adults report having no economics instruction.
- Seven out of ten cannot identify the most widely used measure of inflation.
- More than eight out of ten rate their knowledge of economics as fair to poor.
- Six out of ten do not know the purpose of profits.
- One out of two does not know what the federal deficit is.
- Fewer than half of today's high school seniors have studied economics.
- More than 96% of those surveyed thought schools should teach more about how the economy works.[11]

As I wrote earlier, everyone would be wise to learn more about economics. Every part of money management from small business to the government is based upon economic theories. Knowing economics would give you a much improved ability to take in information and test the facts. That's true for you, and it should motivate you to equip your children with that knowledge as well.

Should Allowance Be Connected to Chores and Tasks?

This is a common question parents have about allowance, and often the starting point for this decision is based on what *their* parents did when they were kids. Did you get an allowance because you had chores to fulfill, or did you receive it just because you were a part of the family? Let's look at both sides.

Attaching allowance to household chores is a popular idea for many parents. They want their children to start learning about how the real world works: an honest wage for an honest day's work. Kids need to learn that money is earned by working, and we hope they learn to work hard and do their best.

Going with this approach, parents might make a list of chores and attach a value to each chore. At the end of the week, they add up the tasks the child has completed and the money associated with them, and that determines the allowance. The basis for this concept is that kids need to learn they earn money for working.

The other common approach is to keep chores and allowance separate. Helping with household chores is expected as part of being a member of the family. Allowance, too, is part of being in the family, and it's viewed more as a tool for teaching children about stewardship. Proponents of this approach believe that kids need to learn that they will always be responsible for certain tasks in life, and they won't be paid for them. Making their bed or helping with dishes are good examples. In adulthood, those are tasks they will need to do, but it's very unlikely that they'll be paid for them.

When I was growing up, my parents actually used both systems. But in our family today, we use the second approach, and that's what I recommend. Although kids need to learn that there are rewards for work, I believe there is plenty of time for them to learn that when they are old enough to work outside the home.

Dad Cents

Also, I see multiple problems with attaching allowance to chores. Remember, allowance is a tool to help you teach your children about managing money. What if kids consistently forget to do their chores, or decide that they would rather not work and not have an allowance? When they get older, maybe they will have enough money for what they want, and decide to skip the chores. And how will they get in a predictable routine if the amount of their allowance changes from week to week? To me, these factors can easily become road blocks to the kids learning about money, which is the main goal.

And for you, keeping records of what they have completed and what they are owed could become a huge headache. If a chore comes along that isn't on the list, you'll have to negotiate a price for getting the kids to help with it. Allowance could quickly become a major source of conflict instead of a learning tool.

I was talking about these different approaches with some friends who have adult children, ages 28 and 30. They told me that, with their kids, they used the second approach—giving allowance separate from chores. They said that during those early formative years, their son and daughter often went beyond the basic requirements of completing tasks, and they continue to do so with their families now.

Listening to my friends talk about this opened my eyes to another big reason not to associate allowance with chores: I don't want my children to grow up with the mindset that they should be paid for everything they do. I want them to be very aware that they can bless others through acts of service, whether it's a family member or a neighbor in need. With this approach, I think they will be more likely to be generous and not always think about what they can get in return for their efforts.

Can we pay a child extra money for extra work? *Absolutely!*

For me, a good guideline is whether I would typically pay someone else to do a job for me—things like raking leaves, shoveling snow (with some help), or cleaning windows, cabinets and closets. Or, maybe you would consider some of these to be expected tasks as part of keeping the household running. There is room for you to customize your approach, but I do believe it's appropriate to pay a child for some things.

How Much Allowance?

Wants, desires and the subject of contentment are all deciding factors in this question. As you instruct your children about contentment, they need to have desires that go unfulfilled. If you give your children everything they want, they will be hard pressed to learn contentment. The amount of allowance should be enough for them to buy some objects they desire, but not all. They should be taught how to save for items that cost more than the spending portion of a week's allowance.

When deciding on the amount, my first recommendation, as with every decision, is to pray and ask God to direct you. I have some suggestions and ideas, but God should be your main source of guidance in this area.

Second, your family must be able to afford the amount. This one may sound obvious, but I think many families are surprised at how quickly the dollars add up over the weeks and months—especially if you need to provide it for three, four, or six children!

Regarding the amount, a common approach is to give a set amount per year of your child's age—50 cents or a dollar for each year, for example. So, an 8-year old would receive $4.00. Then, you will need to decide on frequency: every week, every two weeks, once a month, every time you receive a paycheck, etc.

Dad Cents

Again, I encourage you to find a system that works for you and your family. As an example, one dad I know gives his kids a dollar per year of their age, but gives it to them every 2 weeks. Doing it every week became too much of a chore when it involved finding the right change to split each child's allowance into different percentages for saving, tithing, and so on. (Keep reading for more on that.) Also, for that same reason, he increases their allowance only after their even-numbered birthdays, by two dollars, to make the math a little bit easier. He usually gives out allowances on Sunday morning, so the kids won't have much time to misplace their tithe before they go to church.

One easy way to handle the money side of things is to figure out how much money it would take to cover each child's allowance for the next month or two. Calculate exactly how many $5 bills, $1 bills, quarters, dimes and nickels you'll need, keeping in mind that you'll be setting some percentages aside. Then, make a withdrawal at your bank and request the exact amount of bills and coins needed. (When your children get a little older, you can start giving them their allowance in one amount, then let them figure out how to divide it up for the different categories.)

As you can tell from my examples, *I suggest you give your children their allowance in cash!* In today's world, so many children see their parents pay for everything with a credit or debit card, which gives them skewed ideas about what money is, where it comes from, and where it goes. They need to have experience handling money to learn about the bills and coins. They need to see the actual money being given for the item being purchased to completely grasp what is happening.

Once again, I want to emphasize that your approach with allowance should be motivated by obedience to God and what works best for you and your children.

What Do You Mean I Don't Get All of It?

Do you live on 60% of your income? Why not? More than likely, you were never encouraged to do that or coached on how to make it work. Also, for 99% of middle-class Americans, the answer is simply that they're living beyond their means! The problem is being discontent and trying to keep up with the Joneses. How much of what you use is a need vs. a want? How about all of the things your children have (toys, games, etc.) that they could live without? Are your spending habits and budget set up to live on 60% of your income? If they are, you are out-of-the-ordinary.

I know many of you are not living on 60% of your income, and I know it would be a huge adjustment to switch overnight. But I do believe you will benefit from it, and it's an ideal that you can work toward through the months and years. Stay with me and see if it makes sense to you. For your children, starting them on this plan is a great idea.

Many teens or young adults get the surprise of their life when they get the first paycheck from their first "real" job. After deductions for taxes, FICA, health insurance, a 401k contribution and so on, they're left with only about 70-80% of the gross amount.

Helping your children allocate their allowance into different parts will begin to teach them the 60% rule. I suggest 4 different categories: tithe (giving to church), saving, taxes and spending.

The first 15% (or more, if you want) should go to **giving**. We are to be generous givers, and what better time for your child to begin this habit than at the beginning of his or her experiences with money? Paul says in 2 Corinthians 9:7, "Each one of you should give just as he has decided in his heart, not reluctantly or under compulsion, because God loves a cheerful giver."

Dad Cents

Of the 15% for giving, a good guideline is 10% to the church every Sunday (or as often as they receive an allowance). God's Word is very clear about the priority of giving tithes and offerings: Proverbs 3:9 says, "Honor the Lord from your wealth and from the first fruits of all your crops." Malachi 3:8 gives another clear indication of how important this is: "Can a person rob God? You indeed are robbing me, but you say, 'How are we robbing you?' In tithes and contributions!"

For the other 5%, I suggest placing that in a family offering jar in the house. Once per quarter, sit down as a family and decide on a way to give that money to someone who needs it. In our home, we like to look at the monthly newsletter from the rescue mission. In the late summer, the rescue mission always has a program to help the kids at the mission with school supplies. One time, we took the money in the jar and purchased backpacks full of school supplies for the kids.

Be creative with this, and be sensitive to where God is leading you. There are many projects and causes where you and your family could make a difference. You might help a single mom's ministry, a crisis pregnancy outreach center, a local ministry that helps the disadvantaged in your area, or one of the missionaries your church supports.

Then next 15% goes to **savings**. One prevailing concept in the financial world is to "pay yourself first." That's a way to ensure that you place a priority on saving money for your future. Joshua Kennon, writing in *Investing for Beginners*, puts it this way:

> "You must do this even if you cannot afford it! Then, pay your other bills as usual. If you find that you do not have enough money to cover all the expenses, write down the amount you are short and then find a way to raise the money. If this means you have to recycle cans, switch to an off-brand cereal, work a few extra hours, or cancel your magazine subscriptions, do it."[12]

What could possibly be bad about "paying yourself" 15% for savings? It's wise to save money for emergencies, your next car, your first home purchase, your children's college expenses, and retirement. These are a few of the very logical arguments for "paying yourself first." I have even heard, "Doesn't the Bible say that even the ant stores up provisions?" True, but people often overlook the key word for this concept: *first*. This makes good sense, but the Biblical approach encourages savings to come *second*, not *first*, since giving comes first.

You have probably heard 10% as the suggested percentage of your income to save for retirement, but no one—not even in the investment world—ever gives a valid reason for a 10% savings rate. I believe 15% is a wiser percentage, because at that rate you stand a much better chance of riding out stock market fluctuations and actually having enough money when you need it. If you start listing some of the expenses you're likely to have in the future—and take inflation and other unplanned changes into account—then I think you'll agree that 15% is reasonable. If your child can get accustomed to saving money at this rate, he will have great habits in place when he is out on his own. I realize that, as an adult, you may not be in a 15% savings habit, but I challenge you to work toward that goal.

I'm confident that you understand the reasons for saving money. No one is going to argue with these: emergencies, college, future purchases and retirement are some of the best examples. But you need to be ready to explain some of this to your child when he asks why he doesn't get to spend all of his allowance.

Next, **taxes** are one of the certainties of this world. By beginning early, you can give your children a huge advantage in their understanding of money by having them place 10% into the tax jar.

Okay, I know what you're thinking. "I am not going to

charge my kids taxes!" It isn't really a "tax" like the taxes you pay. The point is really to get your kids used to the idea. You can use the tax jar to fund fun family outings, vacations or fun things for your home for all to enjoy. Decide with your family how and when the tax jar will be used.

In this area, you need to set an example as well. Since you are already paying taxes through a deduction from your paycheck or by another method, you don't need to contribute 10% of your income to the tax jar. But it's appropriate for Mom and Dad to contribute something—maybe an amount that is comparable to, or maybe a little bit higher than, what your children put in the tax jar.

With the remaining 60% of the **allowance**, teaching your children what to do should be easy. They will quickly learn how to spend. And you can sit back and wait for those teachable moments when you can talk about opportunity cost and scarcity. Your kids need to learn good stewardship with that remaining money, but you can encourage them not to feel guilty about spending it. That's part of the beauty of a budget. It's like I used to tell my clients: if you're working with budgeted money and the saving, giving and other expenses are taken care of, there's no need to feel bad about spending what's left.

Now, I want to provide a caution. I don't recommend withholding or reducing your child's allowance as a method for punishing him or her. You want her to see money as a vehicle God desires us to use to show the love that is in our hearts (1 John 3:17). Restricting freedoms such as keeping the television off for a week, limiting computer access, and taking away play time with friends or special toys are all alternative punishment ideas.

On the other hand, I do like an idea that a friend of mine suggested. When your children's irresponsibility or carelessness ends up costing you money or time, it's appropriate to have them pay you back for that—or withhold part of their allowance. For example, if your son neglects to do an assigned chore around the house and your or your wife end up doing it instead, it's reasonable for him to pay you for your time. Or, if your daughter wastes food or toothpaste, or carelessly breaks something that you'll have to replace, she should expect to pay at least part of those expenses. If your child does a poor job of brushing his teeth, he can contribute to what you have to pay to have his cavities filled. This approach will help teach them that there are costs associated with irresponsibility, and we are to be good stewards of what God has provided.

Family Bank

The family banking concept has been around for a long time. Most commonly it looks something like this: Grandpa founded the local bank and then his son became the president and then the grandson succeeded him, and so on. It's a great concept if you're a member of the family.

But that isn't the "family bank" I'm talking about here. I'm referring to a system you can set up in your home for the benefit of teaching your children. It's an idea worth mentioning in case you think it will work for your family.

We are in the process of beginning a bank in which our daughters can deposit their money. This is how the bank works: Allowance is distributed every Friday. Upon receiving allowance, the money will be divided into the appropriate percentage categories. The 5% for family offering and the 10% for taxes will go into the correct jars, and the 10% tithe will be set aside for church on Sunday. The spending money and savings will be deposited into the "Barkley" Bank.

The bank has two accounts for each child: checking and savings. This is a very important part of the concept. The checking account should not pay an interest rate, but the savings account should—at a rate high enough to keep your children interested in saving. Usually, 3% to 6% is a good range—paid each month, and based on the total amount they have saved. You'd probably take that rate in today's times, right? For now, while your child is starting off his savings program, the rate needs to be high so it is noticeable. You can adjust it down when he gets older.

With the two different accounts, your children can get the experience of watching how money grows over time, and compare it to money that's just sitting there, waiting to be spent. The concept of opportunity cost will become more and more evident. They will learn that a larger amount of money in savings will grow more quickly.

Create a spreadsheet to track deposits and withdrawals in the bank, or use one of the online tools at dadcents.com to help you. Make your own checks and deposit slips to help the process.

The family bank brings some teaching benefits that are enormous! Instead of dealing with cash, which makes frivolous spending easier for your children, they have to make deposits and withdrawals into and out of the bank, using the checks and deposit slips. Just like I experienced when working with adults, if your children have to go through an additional step to get to their money, they'll be more likely to rethink a purchase and possibly put it off.

Probably the biggest benefit is that they are more likely to start saving and learn the benefits of saving. Our national savings is at a pathetic rate of about 2%. Increasing our savings rate is the only way to decrease our credit card debt, since money in the bank allows for cash payments for wants and desires as well as emergencies.

The rules for your family bank are up to you. Will you allow borrowing? Are you going to charge interest? Do you want to give your kids an "ATM" card? Does the bank actually have hours, or is it open 24 hours?

As you can see, there are plenty of learning opportunities for your children when it comes to money, and dad, you need to be their number one guide.

Application:

- Start teaching these definitions to your children:

1. Faithful - believing firmly in something or somebody and being consistently trustworthy and loyal, especially to a person, a promise, or duty.
2. Trustworthy - deserving of trust or confidence; dependable; reliable.
3. Accountable - subject to the obligation to report, explain, or justify something; responsible; answerable.
4. To have foresight - the ability to see in advance what may happen and to plan for it.
5. Generous - liberal in giving or sharing; unselfish.
6. Shrewd - showing or possessing intelligence, insight, and sound judgment, especially in business.
7. Effective - producing the intended or expected result.
8. Efficient - performing or functioning in the best possible manner with the least waste of time and effort; having and using knowledge, skill, and industry; competent; capable.
9. Disciplined - Training expected to produce a specific character or pattern of behavior, especially training that produces moral or mental improvement.
10. Content - satisfaction with what one is or has; not wanting more or anything else.
11. Opportunity cost - what must be given up (the next best

alternative) as a result of the decision.

12. Scarcity - a condition of limited resources and unlimited wants and needs.

- Pray and decide if you are going to associate chores with allowance.
- Write down what will be considered chores and what will be considered opportunities for extra money.
- Pray and use guidelines for the amount of allowance for your child(ren).
- Set up a system for allocating and distributing the allowance.

System needs:

1.   A reasonably safe place for taxes, tithe and offerings to be held. It is important that actual money be placed in the container so they can take the physical cash and accomplish the goal for that money.

2.   Percentages to allocate to taxes, tithe, offerings, savings and spending money.

3.   A family bank.

        A. Banking hours and tracking system

        B. Checks and deposit slips

        C. Rates of return for savings

Important – Whatever and however you decide to set up your system, *write it down*. You and your children need to be able to reference the written rules. (There is a reason why God's word is in written form, not just spoken from memory!)

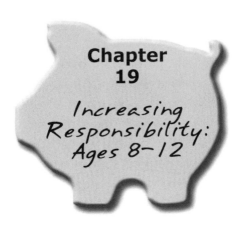

Chapter 19

Increasing Responsibility: Ages 8–12

"The one who deals wisely in a matter will find success, and blessed is the one who trusts in the LORD." Proverbs 16:20

A young and successful executive was traveling down a neighborhood street in his new Jaguar. He was going a bit too fast, but to his credit he was watching for kids darting out from between parked cars. He slowed down when he thought he saw something, but no children appeared. Instead, a brick smashed into the Jag's side door!

He slammed on the brakes and backed up to where the brick had been thrown. The young executive jumped out of the car, grabbed the nearest kid and pushed him up against a parked car, shouting, "What was that all about? That's a new car and the damage from that brick you threw is going to cost a lot of money. Why did you do it?"

The young boy was apologetic. "Please, mister ... please! I'm sorry, but I didn't know what else to do," he pleaded. "I threw the brick because no one else would stop!" With tears dripping down his face and off his chin, the youth pointed to a spot just around a parked car. "It's my brother," he said. "He rolled off the curb and fell out of his wheelchair and I can't lift him up." Now sobbing, the boy asked the stunned executive,

Dad Cents

"Would you please help me get him back into his wheelchair? He's hurt and he's too heavy for me."

Moved beyond words, the young executive tried to swallow the rapidly swelling lump in his throat. He hurriedly lifted the handicapped boy back into the wheelchair, then took out a linen handkerchief and dabbed at the fresh scrapes and cuts. A quick look told him everything was going to be okay. "Thank you and God bless you," the grateful child told the stranger. Too shook up for words, the man simply watched the boy push his wheelchair-bound brother down the sidewalk toward their home.

It was a long, slow walk back to the Jaguar. The damage was very noticeable, but the driver never bothered to repair the dented side door. He kept the dent to remind him to slow down so he could devote more attention to others.

Though my own children aren't there yet, I have many friends who tell me that one of the busiest times of life was when their children were in the 8-12 age range. During that stage, kids are growing and learning rapidly, and the tasks involved in keeping up with them and teaching them what they need to learn adds up to a fast-paced life.

Maybe, like the Jaguar driver, you think you have the situation under control—even while you're speeding along. I hope it doesn't take a brick being thrown into your life for you to see the need to slow down.

In terms of money, children have a way of smashing into the family budget with new and bigger expenses—things they legitimately need, but also things they simply want.

You are entering a time where money decisions can easily become points of contention. The amount of allowance could be an issue, but other matters will almost surely enter the picture as well: they want the more expensive brands of clothing, shoes, and sports equipment; they want to attend movies with their friends many weekends; they need to get something "really good" for that friend whose birthday party they're attending on Saturday; and if they haven't already, they'll start bugging you to get them a cell phone!

Your efforts to train them during these years will be a challenge, but keep in mind that your children need to make some very important steps in their financial education during this phase. The price tags on the objects they want will begin to soar into the hundreds and possibly thousands of dollars. That makes it all the more important that you continue to shape their decision-making abilities for the future with consistent and purposeful direction and training.

Beginning Personal Expenditures

"Dad, will you buy this video game for me?" "Can I have this CD?" I feel confident that you're very familiar with those kinds of pleas. Kids seem to catch on earlier and earlier. And at this age, your children are inundated with appealing advertising and their friends sometimes have nice things that they don't have. And they may have learned by experience that Mom and Dad occasionally give in if they keep asking—their desire for toys, games, clothes and "stuff" seems to grow rapidly.

So, this is why you have regular allowance increases in your plan. One way to fend off arguments about the latest thing your child wants is to simply say, "That does look cool. And in five or six weeks, if you save your allowance, you'll have enough to get it!" Also, if your child is upset about not getting what she wants, that isn't the best time to talk about opportunity cost or scarcity. Save that conversation for another time and simply let the reality of the situation do the teaching.

As you increase your children's allowance, I would suggest that you also increase the number of expenses that they will need to pay for themselves. For example, if you go to a movie as a family, maybe you can pay for the tickets, but if they want a ten-dollar bucket of popcorn, that's up to them. Or if you go to a theme park with your children, you'll pay the admission and the basics like lunch and drinks, but they should expect to pay for souvenirs or extra snacks throughout the day. (And if the trip to the theme park is planned several weeks in advance, it's good to give your children some notice about how this will work.)

In this age range, I don't suggest starting with huge responsibilities. Just to let you know what is coming, in the next two age ranges I recommend moving more and more of your children's budget items to their plate, so they get more money and more responsibility to make purchasing decisions about their clothing, daily care products, and other "normal" expenses. By the time they leave your home, you want them to have plenty of practice making decisions about almost all their financial needs.

With an 8- or 10-year-old, you're just starting down that road, but it's good to keep the end goal in mind and make small changes to move in that direction. As they grow older and their allowance increases, so does their responsibility for expenditures—and their accountability.

Here's an example: Isaac takes his children to the grocery store to purchase the family food for the week. As they traverse the aisles, he asks his daughter Alexa if she would like the name brand or the store brand cereal. Before she can answer, Isaac reminds her that he is willing to buy the store brand, and if she wants the national brand she has to pay the difference. After a short pause, Alexa chooses the store brand.

Alexa's mom, Anna, takes her to shop for school clothes. An outfit at the popular name brand store costs about $35, and a similar one at a discount store (without the popular name on the tag) is about half the cost. After some time looking, Alexa says, "Mommy, these clothes are too expensive! Can we go to the thrift shop?" (No, she is not up for adoption.) This may not sound realistic, but it really does happen when children are trained to think about (once again) opportunity cost, scarcity, and the other principles I've discussed.

As your children start taking more responsibility and growing in their decision-making abilities with money, the requests and begging for things should decrease. Your children will learn that, by saving their money, they have the means to make purchases and don't have to constantly ask you for things. They will probably learn pretty quickly that asking you to buy them things doesn't work! In the process, your children will also begin to make better choices with the money they do have. They'll really start thinking about how much they want something and which things they can live without.

Beginning "Extra Jobs"

When I was about 10 years old, my cousin received a brand new BMX bike for his birthday. When I saw his, of course I wanted one so badly! My old junky bike actually had to be welded together after one of my jumps off a ramp. By the time we were done with the bike, the only original part left was the frame. We had replaced the banana seat (I am showing my age) with a cool black seat. We'd also replaced the wheels, the handlebars and even the rear sprocket so I could freewheel.

So I saved and saved to get my new BMX bike. I did any and every task I could to make extra money—just about any job for which I could talk my parents or anyone else into paying me. When I finally had the new bike, I treated it with great love and care—at least as much as I could as a 10-year-old. I was definitely more careful with my bike than my cousin was with his, and he had received his bike as a gift.

During this stage of life, it's a great time for your kids to learn about extra work. One of my first jobs was weeding a large flower garden for some of our neighbors who were re-tired. That job didn't last very long for me. I complained and grew tired very quickly, and the experience didn't leave me wanting to find another money-making opportunity any time soon.

This brings up an important point about what jobs are best for your child to start with. Notice what your child is good at and interested in, and what he can handle. Does he seem to do better with indoor work or outdoor jobs? Detailed or less detail-oriented tasks? Does he stay with a job for a while, or does his attention wander pretty quickly? Knowing your child's unique gifts and interests will help you greatly, although that doesn't mean you shouldn't still ask him to do something he doesn't enjoy.

Another important point: In the beginning, this process will require quite a bit of your attention. Once your child catches on to the system, he may keep asking you, "What can I do to earn money?" It may be a challenge to come up with tasks that he can handle and that really do make a difference in helping to maintain the household. For example, he may be able to start mowing the lawn at around 12 years of age. (And that will take a lot of your help.) And it can't be something you expect of him anyway as part of being in the family. As I said earlier, a good rule of thumb is that any job you would hire a neighborhood teen to do could be considered an "extra" job.

I would suggest getting together with your wife for a brain-storming session before your child starts asking for ways he can earn money. Come up with a list of jobs that meet your criteria. To get your discussion going, here's a list of tasks you might consider that your child could do in the neighborhood:

- Cleaning windows
- Raking leaves

- Mowing
- Weeding gardens or picking garden produce
- Shoveling snow
- Cleaning windows
- Sweeping patios and sidewalks
- Retrieving mail while the neighbor is on vacation
- Watering lawns, gardens, flowers or houseplants
- Checking on pets for neighbors when they are out of town
- Delivering newspapers
- Sweeping sidewalks of businesses
- Walking dogs
- Selling food and/or drinks when your community has a sidewalk sale or garage sale
- Trimming hedges or bushes
- Cleaning old leaves from plants
- Raking, sweeping or bagging up trimmings for trash collection
- Taking trash and recycle cans to and from the curb
- Handling "pooper scooper" duties

Family Bank Expansion

Expanding the bank concept I described in the previous chapter should occur when your children begin to show more interest in money and its uses. They might start asking questions or trying to look up information on their own. At this point, you might wonder whether to set up a checking account for your child at a real bank. I'm not completely against that, except for the fact that it could get in the way of what you're trying to accomplish with the family bank system.

If the goal is to begin teaching your children how banks work, then I believe the family bank can still do that. It can be set up as extensively as you would like. Your children can have a checkbook to access their money, and that would still require a few steps to get to their money, which would add another chance for them to reconsider their purchase. (As I mentioned before, having easy access to money encourages overspending.) The family bank system will train your children to leave money in the account so it will earn interest. This is why you need to pay them a high interest rate—they need to see the money growing! And that isn't something your kids can get at a regular bank.

By the same token, if you are going to allow loans from the bank, the interest rate you charge should be higher than the rate they are earning on their savings money. The loan process should be an unpleasant experience for them. Take the loan payments directly out of their allowance (an automatic loan payment), and the term of the loan should be very short. Again, it's all about teaching your children lessons about money, and if you can put a bad taste in their mouths about loans because they learn that taking out a loan always costs more in the long run, they'll benefit from that down the road.

Another great lesson your bank can teach is how to reconcile accounts. Your kids have been learning complex addition and subtraction in school, and this will give them good practice. Set up your system so that you can regularly provide them with a summary of checks they have written, and let them manually check to see if their balance matches the "bank."

Financial Concepts

The concepts I suggest for you to emphasize during this stage are probably more familiar to you. Just make sure they also become very familiar to your children.

First, educate your children as to why saving is so important. Here's a great way of looking at it from the National Council on Economic Education:

All decisions involve trade-offs—gaining something and giving something up. People make decisions about spending and saving. If people save, they incur an opportunity cost, the opportunity to satisfy the next most favored want. When people spend, they give up the opportunity to save. In either case, they incur an opportunity cost; and the decision they face is choosing the option with the lower opportunity cost. Over time, savings accumulate into a larger amount. The three reasons for saving are: to purchase a planned good or service in the future; to buy a good or service that people suddenly see and want; and to deal with emergencies and unexpected events.[13]

As you put a savings plan into place, your children will surely ask some pointed questions: "Why do we need to have an emergency fund?" "Why do we need to prepare for the future?" The reasons may seem obvious to you, but please be patient as you give your answers. Children need examples they can relate to. Also, your kids have a very limited concept of time at this stage in their life. They may not have had to replace anything major, or watch you go through the process of paying for a new engine on your car, a new furnace for your home, or some other big expense. They can't really grasp the fact that they will probably need thousands of dollars to go to college in eight or ten years. They probably can't imagine how much money is needed to be able to retire.

There are good everyday examples you can use to explain why saving is important, but don't forget to also give your children biblical reasons. I believe the most compelling answer from Scripture is: so we won't have to borrow money for emergencies or surprise expenses. It goes hand-in-hand with the big principle that capped off the first section of this book: contentment. If we "have learned the secret of being content in any and every situation" (Phil. 4:12), then our children are better prepared to make saving a priority. Living within our means and saving a portion of our income is absolutely necessary. It's simply wise stewardship to trust God first but also to be prepared for emergencies. How much should we set aside? I believe a good figure is enough to cover 3 to 6 months of living expenses.

What about saving for the future? I suppose this is where many people would use the word "retirement," although the Bible says nothing about that concept. Regardless, many of us have goals and dreams for our later years, when we hope to make some changes to our work schedules and obligations. For many, that's also a time when they get even more involved in ministry opportunities.

Going back to the question about how much, the answer is a bit more difficult—partly because different people have different dreams, and they define their wants and needs in different ways. So I recommend seeking God's wisdom on this question. Think realistically about how much savings you will need later in life, and ask Him to give you a comfort level with an amount that is not hoarding, but is not irresponsible. Then, once you have that monthly amount to allocate to savings, it's time to be faithful, shrewd, efficient, effective, accountable and disciplined with that money.

As I said, your children may not grasp all of the issues you are considering when you save, but they will learn from watching you and seeing the results of your savings. If you cannot explain to your children why you are saving, they will have difficulty grasping the concept for themselves.

On their level, it's good for them to be able to watch their savings growing—with interest—and even benefit from the savings at some point, whether they buy a car or a computer for school with money they have saved, or they make a major contribution to their college tuition bill.

The goal is to keep your children from being dependent upon financial institutions. Sometimes we can benefit from the valuable services those financial companies provide, but we want to keep from being in a position where we have to rely on them. We should be relying on God and His principles first and foremost.

The other two concepts for this stage, which are best taught together, are supply and demand. Understanding these terms is a key to being shrewd, having foresight and being content. The price for goods or services has a direct correlation to supply and demand. Again, here's a description from Investopedia. com:

> Supply and demand is perhaps one of the most fundamental concepts of economics and it is the backbone of a market economy. Demand refers to how much (quantity) of a product or service is desired by buyers ... at a certain price.... Supply represents how much the market can offer ... the amount of a certain good producers are willing to supply when receiving a certain price.... Price, therefore, is a reflection of supply and demand.[14]

Here are a few examples that should help: the Apple iPhones created an amazing buzz in the technology world and with many 15-to-45-year-old guys—people like me. The new device did just about everything: phone, internet, email, music, videos, a calendar and pictures. An amazing phone, right? I had to remind myself, "Hey, wait a minute. The phone I have does all of those same things!" Quite a few phones already on the market could do almost everything the iPhone did.

Still, discontent Americans stood in long lines and paid high dollar for those new phones. Some people reportedly waited in line for 100 hours, and many bought the phone to simply resell

Dad Cents

it on the Internet. Others made $250 per day to stand in line to buy the phone for people who had other obligations.

Did anyone wonder if the limited supply of iPhones was a marketing ploy? Did Apple really have a problem making enough for everyone? Supply and demand is the answer. Low supply plus high demand equals high price!

You may remember a similar phenomenon with Xbox 360 and the PS3 video game consoles. Initially, people were buying the Xbox 360 on the Internet for up to $2,000 per machine! The law of supply and demand can either cost you a significant sum of money or make you a significant sum of money. Your knowledge will determine the outcome.

Another example of supply and demand is reflected in gasoline prices. In the past few years, prices reached an all-time high, forcing people to cut back on how much they were traveling, find alternate transportation options, and so on. Essentially, the demand for gas was reduced. Assuming the supply remains steady—no hurricanes damage offshore oil refineries and the oil workers don't go on strike, for example—then the price will go down.

There are examples like this around us all the time and my point is simply that we need to talk about these concepts with our children when we have the opportunity. A series of 30-second comments from you through the years could really help set your children ahead of the crowd in their understanding of economics and how to navigate the world of money.

Application:

- Begin the next step in growing your children's understanding of the key concepts we have covered:

  1. Faithful – Do not miss any of your children's allowance

payments. They need to see you regularly give them their allowance.

2. Trustworthy – Have clear expectations that your children are to finish their chores every week.

3. Accountable – Make your children responsible to finish for their chores on a regular basis.

4. Foresight - Have the children help plan the family vacation. Allow them to watch the "tax" money grow to help their anticipation of the trip.

5. Generosity – Be creative with your offering money. Look at the needs list of your local rescue mission or other ministries, buy what you can from the list, and take the items to the mission.

6. Shrewd – Read a story of a financially successful person and share some of the concepts from the book with your children.

7. Effective – Only pay your child for the job when the desired result is accomplished!

8. Efficient – Pay your child by the job, not by the hour. They need to see they have the opportunity to make more money by working hard to get done.

9. Disciplined – Tell your children about a new family vehicle or other item for which you are saving. Let them see you save the money and then pay cash for the expenditure.

10. Content – Help your children understand supply and demand. Teach them to be patient (to remain content) when it comes to high-demand items and wait until prices go down.

11. Opportunity Cost – Your children should understand that when they choose one item, they do not get the other choices.

12. Scarcity – Your children are beginning to want things

(games, toys) that cost more than their allowance provides. Explain that scarcity (not having enough money) is why they need to begin saving.

13. Savings – The family bank should help provide learning. Your children should begin seeing accumulation in their account. This growth will be a great encouragement.

14. Supply & Demand – (See content above.) Help your children see that by waiting they are able to purchase more, after the prices go down.

- Start giving your child some responsibility for making small purchasing choices, such as food items, and gradually increase the responsibility to shoes or clothing as he or she moves closer to the age of 12.
- Decide how much to increase your children's allowance to correlate with the increased responsibility of making their own purchases.
- Be very clear about what is expected (as part of the family) and the work that is to be considered "extra" (jobs they can expect to be paid for).
- Encourage your child to pursue "extra" jobs so they can save for more expensive items (video games, toys, clothes) they want.
- Make a list of potential "extra" jobs your kids can do to earn money, and post the job list for encouragement.
- Continue to encourage and develop the family bank.
- If you are going to loan money, make strictly defined rules.

1) Payment amount
2) Interest rate
3) Payment frequency
4) Collateral – something of great value they own
5) Default ramifications

- ***Write down everything***!
- Learn, learn, and learn about economics and how our country's economy works with or against one's personal economy. Take a class at a community college, your public library or online. Make our economy work for you (and your children) instead of you working for the economy.

Chapter 20

The Big Picture: Ages 12-15

"Train a child in the way that he should go, and when he is old he will not turn from it." Proverbs 22:6

"Hey, Josh," said Dave the UPS delivery guy. "Did you buy some more soccer gear?" "Yeah," said Josh. "Some shorts and shoes." Josh and Dave knew each other on a first name-basis. Dave delivered items that Josh purchased on the Internet or by mail order to take advantage of lower prices compared to the local soccer and sporting goods shops.

Why was Josh so interested in saving money? Because his parents allotted him a monthly budget for clothing and other expenses. Josh was able to have clothing and equipment similar to his friends without spending nearly as much money. And in many cases, he didn't care to have the brands his friends had anyway. All that stuff mattered less and less to him now.

Because his parents gave him money to work with and challenged him with a budget, he learned to be very efficient with his money, and he learned to be content with what he had. Those skills served him well through college, and today, as a young married man, he still benefits from those lessons learned as a teenager.

A wise friend of mine who is also the CFO of a large company tells me that the time period when our children are ages 12-15 is tremendously important due to the limited number of teachable moments we have with them. "One day you will have a heart-to-heart, lucid conversation," he said, "and the next day you will speak to them and they'll be on another frequency—no chance to have comprehensible dialogue."

His comment helps to reinforce the idea that this stage of life for kids is often difficult—for the children and the parents. (Maybe more difficult for the parents!) We have to make the most of every opportunity that presents itself to influence our children toward responsibility and good stewardship.

In terms of money, this stage is very significant. Several key changes occur for your children—including the capacity to handle more financial resources and to become more independent in the use of those funds.

From Allowance to "Salary"

With kids this age, there is no change in the principles we teach them, but there is a slight change in the approach. Or maybe we could say it's a different mind set. Now we start thinking of that regular money as a "salary" instead of an allowance.

As I mentioned in an earlier chapter, I am *not* recommending that you start associating this money with work that your children do; it isn't a salary in that sense. But it is a definitive amount of money that is received at regular intervals. And, like you probably do with your paychecks, your children have an opportunity to use that money to start paying for more of their living expenses. So, "salary" is a good term and a good method to use as you continue teaching them about money. They will learn to be efficient, effective and shrewd as they continue the journey toward independence.

Clearly, this approach will mean significant increases in the amount you give them when you hand out allowances. Your children can gain experience and learn stewardship using everyday needs and living expenses. How do you determine the amount of money to give them for all of the different expenses they are expected to cover? Set up a budget! That gives them guidelines and limits what they have to spend.

Becoming familiar with budgeting is an important step for your children. They're managing larger sums of money, and if they have unlimited resources, they will have no reason to limit their wants. They won't develop self-control and they will learn nothing—except maybe years later, from the school of hard knocks. But if you have been teaching and modeling the concepts of opportunity cost, scarcity, and supply and demand, this is when they get to start practicing what they have learned.

How much money is appropriate for your teen's "salary"? Many factors influence that decision, including patterns you have set up in previous years, your current budget, and specific knowledge of your unique child—how much money and which spending decisions you believe he or she can handle.

Beyond those individual factors, the first step to setting your children's salary is determining what expenses they will be responsible for paying out of the salary. A good guideline here is to give them enough money to cover the expenses you set forth, but not enough to buy whatever they desire or to spend the money frivolously.

Whether or not you use the salary approach, deciding how much you will pay for a particular expense is an important step. Then, if your child wants a particular brand or model of something that's more expensive—clothing, shoes, cosmetics, ice cream, or whatever—they pay the "excess" amount out of their allowance or other personal funds. For example, if you're using the salary system and you've allotted $50 per month to clothing, but your child wants running shoes that cost $100, then he needs to find a way to come up with the rest of the money. (If you aren't on the salary system, you simply tell him how much you're willing to pay for a suitable pair of running shoes, and then he pays the difference.) If your budget for your daughter allows $2.50 for shampoo and she "needs" a brand that costs $10, then she pays the difference or finds a way to make it work given the other expenses that need to be paid out of her salary.

Here are some basic ways I see the salary playing out at this age:

Shelter & Personal Needs: This includes rent or mortgage payments, utilities, insurance, and so on. Dad and Mom should continue to handle these payments.

At this age, I would suggest including personal hygiene items in this category—paid for by Dad and Mom. Generally speaking, boys might have problems keeping deodorant, toothpaste, and similar items on hand, and this probably isn't an area where you want to let them get into bad habits. Girls will probably care more about personal hygiene at this age, but they may also be tempted to buy the most expensive brands. You know your children best, so you can add hygiene items to their salary at the right time.

Food: There is plenty of room for you to customize your approach here. Does this part of the salary include all the food they eat? At home and at restaurants? Are school lunches included? What about candy and snacks? Or when they are getting pizza with friends? Decide what food you will pay for, and then involve your child in determining how much he will probably need as you discuss the above questions. Just be clear about how much he is responsible to pay.

Clothing: I recommend including all of your child's clothing in the salary. For some of you, it may sound much too soon for this, but clothing is a great area in which your child can begin making choices and learning from them. Simply determine an appropriate amount by reviewing your budget from last year, or sit down with your wife and use your best guess regarding what your child will need. Then give him or her the money—and the responsibility. Be flexible at first, and be ready to tweak the amount in this category if you need to. Also, make sure to explain to your child that she will probably need to save some of the clothing budget for school clothes in August. That's often a big expenditure.

As your child becomes more observant and starts thinking more creatively with her purchases, you might make some money-saving suggestions for her clothing purchases. For example, she could buy "pre-owned" brand-name clothing from local stores, consignment sales, or online; she could sell some items for a small profit when she doesn't need them anymore; she could save for after-Christmas sales or end-of-season mark-downs, or use coupons that come in the mail or news-paper. You and your wife probably know other money-saving options in your area.

One other option, instead of selling the clothes, is to donate them to a local rescue mission or other out-reach. You might consider paying your child a small amount for the clothes she donates, to offset what she won't earn since she isn't selling them, and to increase the reward she receives from the gesture. My wife and I do this regularly with some of our clothing. I remember a jacket of my grandfather's which my dad gave to me when my granddad passed away. It was too big for me, but I couldn't bring myself to give it away. Finally, God showed me that the coat could be useful to someone else, and I donated the coat. A few months later, I was back at the mission and saw a gentleman wearing my grandfather's coat. Needless to say, I knew I had made the right decision.

Entertainment / Personal Spending: The previous categories are generally needs, but this one is all about wants! It's important to get this one right, and I suggest you and your wife make this decision together—when your child is not around. You want to make sure he has enough to do some fun things and have opportunities to learn wisdom in this area too. Is this already provided for in your child's allowance? Should your child be expected to earn extra money for this category? One factor to consider is how much you would give your child if you were still making the decisions with the money. I believe a good compromise is to allocate *some* money to this category, but also have your child make money with "extra" jobs if he wants more. (Keep reading for more on that.)

Extras: There are other expenses I haven't mentioned that you will run into, such as getting your child a cell phone. Another example: maybe you pay for fees and equipment for your kids' sports, music, or dance activities, but your child wants to add another activity that isn't in your budget. That's something she might be expected to pay. As always, you'll want to carefully consider these.

Believe it or not, dad, determining the salary is relatively easy compared to what comes next: actually allowing your child to control the money. It's tough to sit back and watch your child make foolish choices. Our natural desire as parents is to spare our children from pain, even if it's due to their own poor choices. But it's very important for them to make those mistakes and learn some of those hard lessons while still under your roof. Remember, if they can learn a valuable lesson now and it costs them ten or 20 dollars, that's much better than having them learn that lesson ten years from now, when it might cost them hundreds or even thousands.

For the same reason, you have to resist bailing them out when they have squandered their money. This too is very difficult. If a child has no money left because he spent it frivolously, and then his friend calls and wants to go see a movie, don't give him the money for the movie and don't let him pay you back out of his next salary payment. He needs to experience the consequence and stay home. Only bail him out in an extreme emergency.

Now, some of you may be questioning this approach. Is it bad stewardship or wasting money to let your kids make poor decisions? No, all my research tells me that it's an investment in your children's future to educate them and give them these experiences using money. And remember, the amount you are giving your children is budgeted; it's what you would be spending on them anyway.

I Am Responsible for What Budget?

When I was 15 years old, my parents told my sister and me that we would be getting a budget for clothing. The monthly budget was to be $50 per month. In the mid 80's, that was much more than I needed, but apparently that's how much was in their budget. Being extremely tight with my money at that age (and my wife would tell you nothing has changed), I asked my parents what happened to the money I didn't spend. They told me I could keep whatever I didn't need for clothing. Wow!

Suddenly my clothes had a much longer shelf life than before.

That decision by my parents gave me many learning opportunities as I managed my clothing allowance. Maybe a bigger benefit was the example they set for me. They had a family budget, and though I didn't see everything, I got a good glimpse of how it worked. They also allowed me to make some decisions within that structure. The budget allowed me to live within my means and helped me learn to make godly choices when decisions came.

Living within a budget is a skill that very few people in our country possess, but it's extremely important to set up a budget for your family. You can do it, and your modeling is the best way for your children to learn this facet of finances. When they leave home with that ability, you will have given them the foundation for the wise use of God's money in their lives.

On the next page is a sample budget for a child's monthly salary. As you look it over, remember that it's just an example of how this works. The amounts in the various categories might not reflect your values, and that's fine. I expect you to do what fits with your budget and your standard of living. Also, this exercise should not increase the amount you're paying for anything; the salary should be based on what you're already spending for these things. This approach simply shifts the responsibility for the spending decisions to your child.

The Big Picture

Monthly Salary	$ 175.00	Actual Expenditures
Clothing	$25.00	
School	$25.00	
Athletics	$25.00	
Food	$25.00	
School lunches	$50.00	
Friends	$25.00	
Entertainment/ Personal	**$50.00**	
Savings	$7.50	
Tithe	$5.00	
Offerings	$2.50	
Taxes	$5.00	
Misc. personal spending (video games, toys and stuff he/she wants, time with friends, etc)	$30.00	
Budget Total	**$225.00**	

I have more budget forms available at www.dadcents. com.

One important note: Savings, tithe, offerings and taxes are still the same percentages that I mentioned earlier, but are based on the dollar total in the entertainment/personal category, not the entire salary total. The entertainment/personal category of the salary is essentially the same as the allowance.

Also, the learning process here is based on allowing your child to make decisions. So, if he wants to move money from one category to another for a particular need or want, that's fine. If he doesn't spend all his clothing money, he can add what's left to his food or personal spending totals. If he eats light during school lunches and doesn't spend all of his money in that category, he can spend that money on something else. Of course, you should make it clear that he may not do that with the monthly amounts for tithe, savings, offering and taxes. He needs to learn self-discipline in those areas.

How Can I Make Extra Money?

I remember the first time I had a paying job where I was not working for my parents or next-door neighbor. A friend from church had a small farm and needed some help with chores. I would go over on Saturday morning and do all kinds of jobs that I had never done before. It was a valuable experience for me, although I quickly discovered a few tasks that I did not want as part of my career. In a similar way, this is a good time for your kids to start those kinds of jobs. Those work opportunities provide your kids with some extra cash, which they want, and they provide lessons about responsibility. Also, it's amazing how teens are usually more responsible with and take better care of things they have bought with their own money.

At a certain point, your kids will run out of ways to make extra money at home—or you'll run out of jobs and money to pay them. Maybe they want different jobs or greater earning opportunities, so they will start looking outside your home. My first business venture was mowing yards. I started with people in our neighborhood, and once I had a car, the sky was the limit.

More potential jobs:

- Window washing
- Mowing
- Baby-sitting
- Painting
- House cleaning
- Caring for pets / walking dogs
- Helping people move
- Tutoring
- Running errands
- Washing or detailing cars
- Selling items on eBay
- Setting up and maintaining an Internet store
- Shoveling snow
- Delivering papers
- Teaching computer skills
- Creating web sites

This list is a small portion of the possibilities, but it should help get your kids' minds working on ways to make extra money.

As they begin work for people outside of your family, one of your roles is to help coach them. What does it mean to do their best? What makes for a job well done? Why is it important to show up on time? They need to learn about concepts like expectations, excellence, and what it means to work at something "with enthusiasm, as to the Lord and not for people, because you know that you will receive your inheritance from the Lord as the reward" (Colossians 3:23-24).

Using the example from my youth, when I mowed and trimmed a neighbor's yard, what was the yard expected to look like when I finished? My standard was (and still is) no stray strands of grass sticking up, the edging done around all of the sidewalks and the street, and the extra clippings blown or swept off the sidewalk and driveway. My wife's expectations, on the other hand, are quite different! (And to be fair, my cleaning expectations are not like hers either. I'll let you guess about the specifics on that.) But you can see how there are many opportunities for coaching your kids.

Another part of that coaching is to let them practice their jobs at home. Allow them to mow your lawn, wash your car, shovel your drive or paint your fence, so you can talk specifically about standards, expectations, and doing their best. I know you are thinking: *Free labor!* Make sure to pay them as would be expected anywhere else.

One important point about this money that they are earning: This isn't "mad money" that is theirs to spend however they please. The money from outside work goes into the personal expenditure category, and they take out the appropriate percentages for savings, tithe, offerings and taxes.

The Stock Market

"Mr. Bodenheimer, Mr. Wisdom's class has a stock market game that they can use to invest money. Would you start a stock market game in our class?" I asked. Mr. Bodenheimer replied, "Shane, if you want to organize a stock market game and be the stock broker, that would be fine with me."

This conversation (or something very similar) happened between me and my 6th grade teacher, and that began my interest in finances. Our class had a money system where the teacher rewarded or penalized students for grades and behavior. I learned pretty early that my money could work for me and increase the return on my efforts, so it was as if there were two of me making money. Consequently, I learned how to be a broker and we started a stock market game.

I suggest you try a system much like the one we used in 6th grade: Begin by explaining the big picture of how the stock market works to your kids. (If you don't feel very educated about the stock market, do some homework.) From there, you have two options: use pretend money to teach the concepts—which will still educate them about how the market works—or use real money.

If you choose to use real money, then you will be responsible for paying the profits, as well as taking in any losses. Depending on how aggressive your children decide to be, generally their losses will offset most of the gains you would have to pay. If you do go with this approach, once your kids understand the basic concepts, have them decide on an amount of money they want to invest—*an amount that they could stand to lose.* You may be surprised that I used that wording. But it's appropriate with the stock market, and that's what your children need to experience. The market rises and falls due to numerous events: oil shortages, war, terrorist attacks, good or bad government reports, supply and demand, and sometimes for no visible reason at all! Some stocks have a general trend upwards in price, but there is no guarantee that any stock will remain at its current price.

Once your son or daughter has decided on the amount of money to allocate to the market, start tracking some different companies. Use a notebook or a spreadsheet to track purchases and sales of stocks. Have your son/daughter calculate the prices, shares and money related to the transactions. Use the close-of-day price for your purchases and sells. The closing prices are very easy to find on the Internet or in a newspaper. If the selling price is higher than the purchase price, they can sell their position and make a profit. If they sell below the purchase price, they will lose money. I would recommend using real money until they start making profits that you cannot afford to pay.

Also, while I do recommend telling your children about broker's fees and the costs of investing, I would be very hesitant to actually charge your children fees. They need to have fun and learn about the market at this point, and the more profit they make, the more motivated they'll be to keep investing (and keep learning).

One more thing: If setting up your own stock market sounds too involved for you and your family, there are also games available on the Internet that allow mock stock purchasing and selling. Do a quick online search and you'll find plenty of options.

If you're familiar with investing, you know I can't do the topic justice in a book of this length. So let me urge you to do more reading on the topic. At www.dadcents.com I have provided a list of books and other resources that have been very useful to me in this area.

Financial Concepts

The Luxury Marketing Council of Florida says that luxury spending has seen an annual growth of 20-30%, where general retail spending has seen an increase of 5%. The definition of *luxury* by the Encarta Dictionary is "an item that is desirable but not essential, and often expensive or hard to get.[15]" Translation: *needs* are up 5% per year, and *wants* are up 20-30%!

One of the most challenging traps that Satan sets for our children (and for us) is convincing us that our wants are really needs. But if we can keep this straight, we'll be well on our way toward living with the "secret" I mentioned earlier: contentment.

A need is very Biblical. In Matthew 6:25-34, Jesus tells us not to worry because God takes care of even the flowers and the birds, so he will definitely provide for our needs. So what is a **need**? Food, shelter and clothing. Generations of people have lived with very little money—only a fraction of what most of us live on. That's the baseline for where we start talking about needs. Living on very little money is not fun, and that desire for an easier life or the things other people have is what Satan uses to create wants.

Obviously, **wants** are things that we would like to have. Usually wants come disguised as needs. I need clothes, and this name brand that is 50% more expensive will make me cool. Kids want to fit in with classmates. The problem is that the cheaper clothes provide the same basic benefit. They provide protection against the weather conditions.

I don't have a problem with name-brand clothing, especially when I can buy the clothing at the same price as the generic or discount store option. By shopping around and being patient, I can often find name-brand items—Nike athletic socks or Polo button-up shirts, for example—just as inexpensively as comparable options that are generic. Also, as I wrote earlier, it's appropriate to account for the difference in quality during the decision-making process.

Because of advertising, peer pressure or a range of other factors, we too easily blur the lines between needs and wants. We convince ourselves that our wants are really needs. I guess I'm talking about us dads now. But again, our children are watching and learning from what we do. Raising our children with a healthy awareness of their needs and wants means addressing this question ourselves. Give God full access to your financial decisions and priorities. He really *already has* full access, but it's good for us to intentionally submit ourselves to Him in this area.

I believe God wants us to live joy-filled lives, and He allows us some material pleasures now and then. But we should be cautious not to use that as an excuse to go overboard. We should seek His will regularly about whether we're pleasing Him with our stewardship.

Then, we should start having regular conversations with our kids as teachable moments come around. Whenever they use the word "want" or "need" in reference to something, question them on why they used that word. Is it *really* a need, or a very strong desire? What likely caused that desire? Then, there's the difficult question that we need to make sure we're also asking ourselves: What would Jesus say about wants and needs in this situation?

If your children can get a good grasp of the difference between needs and wants, it will be a big benefit to them for the rest of their lives. The concept is so simple, yet so complex. We can usually communicate the ideas pretty simply, but applying the ideas to real-life wants becomes very complex.

Application:

- Begin the next steps in growing your children:

  1. Shrewd – Teach your kids how to shop wisely, whether for clothes, electronics or other needs. Help them find discount stores such as liquidators and search the Internet for their purchases.
  2. Faithful / Trustworthy – Use your kids' extra jobs to teach them to be faithful and trustworthy. Make sure they understand the importance of showing up and following through on whatever job they have.
  3. Efficient – Your kids should have learned this by working for you, but it can be reinforced with extra jobs. The more efficient they are, the more shoveling, mowing or cleaning they can accomplish, and the more money

they can make.

4. Effective – As your children begin to work for other people, inspect their work so they can learn generally accepted standards. Give them a good feel for the desired results.

5. Accountable – Do not bail out your child if he is irresponsible with his budget.

6. Generosity – Help your kids find out what a local ministry or non-profit organization needs, then contribute to help meet those needs (e.g., buy some items that the church youth group needs and secretly place them in the meeting room or youth pastor's office. It is great fun to see someone wonder where something came from.)

7. Content – Every 3 months, take inventory of your kids' money and allow them to keep the budget money that they do not spend. You might be amazed how content your kids can be with what they already have!

8. Disciplined – Use income from extra jobs to teach discipline. Make sure your children allocate the correct percentages to savings, tithe, offerings, and taxes. They need to do this every time they receive money!

9. Foresight – Use the budget to talk about future expenditures. School clothing is probably the best example. Your children need to start saving some of the monthly budget for next August.

10. Opportunity Cost – As the budget grows and more responsibility is added, your child will be required to make more choices. Watch how she chooses and provide encouragement for good decisions.

11. Scarcity – Your teens are beginning to work odd jobs for others and over the summer. They may have more personal spending money than you do. Monitor their in-

come and steer them toward good decisions. They have unlimited wants, and problems can arise if they are able to spend this money with no accountability.

12. Savings – New savings goals can help with the previous concern. Encourage your child to save for a big-ticket item he has been wanting, like a computer. His participation in big purchases will begin to teach independence.

13. Supply & Demand – Help your child learn to use eBay, where she can purchased items at great savings over retail prices. She can try an item and then resell it on eBay for a comparable price or a small profit.

14. Wants vs. Needs – Model and teach your children the difference between wants and needs. When you shop for groceries or clothing, pick out two items that are virtually the same except for the brand name. Talk about the difference in price and which one you want versus which one will meet your need.

- Get started switching from allowance to salary. Be as accurate as possible on budget categories. If category amounts are too big, your teens will not need to be efficient with their money.

- Build a budget sheet. Use envelopes to designate the different budget categories. Put cash into the envelopes every month. Then **let your teens manage the money**. Show them how to track where they spend the money. Make a column on the budget sheet to write the item and where the purchase was made.

- Have contests with your kids to see who can find the best deals. Show them how to search the Internet for their purchases. Audit their books every three months and allow them to keep any leftover money. (You might see how the budget numbers go for 3-6 months before announcing this to your kids.)

- Look at your children's abilities and help them decide what extra jobs to pursue. Help them learn to do the jobs well. Also, let them buy their own equipment and have ownership. If the job is lawn mowing, they should work toward having their own mower.

- Read a generalized book about the stock market. Help your children experience successes (and some failures) in the market. Success breeds interest, and interest knowledge. If you need help, ask someone at church.

- Teach the difference between needs and wants. Tell your kids they could have $100 and water, or $1 million and no water. Most kids would choose the $1 million. Ask them what they would do with $1 million when they are dead? They *need* water to live, but they *want* $1 million.

Chapter 21

Last Chance: Ages 15-18

"How much better it is to acquire wisdom than gold; to acquire understanding is more desirable than silver." Proverbs 16:16

I sure need a car to get to all of my practices and all of the other school and church events, I thought to myself. Maybe I was blurring the boundary between "needs" and "wants," as we discussed in the last chapter. It was definitely a want, and I was out to convince Mom and Dad that it was also a need. My parents finally agreed when I was 15 years old. That may seem a little young, but it was pretty normal here in the Midwest. And remember, the city where I grew up had only about 120,000 people.

Like many teenagers, I had a busy schedule. I played one sport or another during every season of the year. One summer I played over 100 baseball games. In the mostly rural area where we lived, the transportation options were a bicycle or hitching a ride with a friend or family member.

I began my car search with high hopes and quickly discovered that I could afford much less than I had thought. I had about $600 saved, and my dad offered to match that amount toward a car. After what seemed like a long search, finally the car of my dreams (the one I could afford) was in the newspaper. I took my dad to look at the car, and after driving the car and having a mechanic friend give it a quick inspection, we plopped down the $1200. It was a 1976 Chevy Monza! She sure was pretty. Well, not really, but she was all mine.

The First Car

Get ready for any and every argument from your teenager about why he or she "needs" a car. Then, stay ready, because if you don't agree to that first request, it will surely be followed by another ... and another. Eventually, for whatever reasons, you'll start giving the idea some real consideration. It's a big decision that needs to be made carefully.

Below are eleven questions that you will want to think about, research, and pray about during this process—and you may have others you'll want to add to the list. Write down your thoughts and decisions about these:

1. Who will pay for the initial purchase of the car?
2. Who will pay for the maintenance—oil, tires, windshield wiper blades, engine repairs, etc.?
3. Who will pay for the gas? I grew up writing down my mileage on the odometer, the date, gallons and cost at each fill-up in a small notebook kept in the car. This method helped tremendously in tracking the dollars spent on gas. Here's another related question: Are you willing to pay for gas if your child uses the car to run errands such as groceries?
4. Who will pay for the tags & taxes? This could be very important, depending upon the state where you live.
5. Who will pay for insurance? This is a huge consideration. Insurance premiums alone could help you decide the kind of car that you purchase. Adding a teenage driver to your insurance could raise your premiums by up to

200%, so make sure you check on good student discounts and what the stipulations are for that program. Another must when your kids begin to drive is to add an umbrella liability policy to your coverage. Their own safety is your biggest concern, but from an insurance perspective, the largest risk when your children begin to drive is the possibility of them injuring someone else. An umbrella policy will significantly reduce your risk, for only pennies on the dollar.

6. Who pays for violations—speeding, parking etc.?

7. Who pays for accidents?

8. Who is allowed to ride in the car, and how many at a time? What other activities are forbidden for your child while he/she is driving? (Listening to music? Talking on a cell phone? Eating and drinking?) Some kind of restriction here is a must, and in some states the decision is already made for you. For example, in the state of Maryland, it's now illegal for someone under 18 to:
   - Get a ride to school with your friend.
   - Answer a phone call while driving.
   - Drive your date to the movies.
   - Check a text message while driving.
   - Be a designated driver.[16]

Make sure to check your state laws! Along with that, you know your child and what he can handle. Knowing how easily people are distracted by some of these things—and given the fact that your teen is an inexperienced driver—I would recommend being pretty strict on these in the beginning. You can always relax the rules later as your child demonstrates responsibility.

9. Who owns the car? This question is bigger than it may

appear. Ownership of the car may be important in determining how your child views your ability to restrict or take away car privileges, where he can go, how long he can be away from home, and so on. In my view, these are significant responsibilities that need to be grown into.

10. What type of consequences will come into play if your teen is irresponsible with the car?

11. Are driving trips outside school, athletics and work subject to prior approval?

If you decide to pay for some or all of the car expenses, make sure you add a section to your budget just for the car. Also, discuss what happens if your child exceeds his budget in this area, and who is responsible.

I'm sure you know that cars are some of the bigger expenses in life. Between purchasing, gas, maintenance and insurance, they can take a huge chunk of the budget. Also, cars are depreciating assets; they cost you money! Rarely can you sell a car for more than you paid for it.

It's good to have a balanced perspective on the whole situation. Really, a car is a way to get from one place to another. I say this as a reformed "caraholic." In the past 19 years, I have owned 27 cars and trucks! To say that I am somewhat familiar with negotiating for a car and all of the other details is an understatement. Safety and reliability are worth something, but the basic purpose of a car is to transport you and/or your child from one place to another. Getting caught up in specific makes and models or extra features is usually not healthy for your budget.

Decisions made in this area of transportation can make a significant impact on your children's future. And your modeling will be crucial in molding your child's view.

A Real Job!

For many teens, a job is a major step toward independence. Having a job might be one good reason for needing a car, unless other transportation options are available. Typically, teenagers work for two reasons: they want to or they have to.

I believe the best option is to keep your teenagers from working during the school year. Multiple studies concluded that students who work perform at a lower level in school than those who do not work. A study by John H. Taylor in the *Journal of Labor Economics* found that students who reduced their work during the school year by ten hours per week increased their math scores by a ".2 standard deviation."[17]

But during the summer months, of course, work is a great option—provided that it doesn't interfere with family plans, since summer also brings many opportunities for memory-making family trips and events. When I was in high school, I always made enough money over the summer to pay for gas, oil, insurance and taxes for my car. With some planning—and possibly some help from you—your child can probably earn enough through the summer so he won't need to work during the school year.

I encourage you to look back at the job lists I provided in the previous two chapters. For your teen, those can become a major source of income. The jobs that worked best for me were mowing, painting and cleaning. They allowed some flexibility in my schedule, and I made more money than I could have if I had worked at the mall or a grocery store.

If your child decides to start his own businesses—whether it's mowing, painting, or something else—that's a great learning tool, and you can be part of that. I suggest speaking with a certified public accountant (CPA) about deductions and other possible issues that could arise. You can also coach your child to keep careful track of his expenses. This is very important!

Sometimes the dollars people spend to set up and run the business offset the income of the business.

What Taxes?

By now, your teenagers are probably familiar with the concept of taxes, and they won't be too shocked at the amount that's taken out for taxes and other deductions if they work at an hourly job. If you have been following along and using the concepts in the preceding chapters, your teenager understands that she will not receive 100% of her paycheck. She knows that taxes are a fact of life.

If she is shocked, sit down with her and go over the family budget again. You may not want to show her everything, but showing her what you pay in taxes and other regular expenses will enlighten her about the amount of money needed to run the household, and about the reality of taxes.

Of course, learning about taxes also includes filing a tax return each spring. Your child should be able to file a 1040 EZ if she is working on an hourly basis. My parents ran a daycare out of our home, so my father helped me learn how to file a self-employed tax return. As I ventured into the financial consulting business, years of filing my own taxes greatly increased my understanding of taxes and was a tremendous advantage. If you're uninformed about taxes or uncomfortable with doing them yourself, I highly recommend getting help from a CPA. That qualified help is a tremendous asset.

Integrating Work with Salary

The last step while your teenager is at home is integrating his work money with the salary you provide. This is another step in the shift of responsibility to his shoulders, and it's based on the income he is able to generate, whether he works over the summer or all year 'round.

You should continue to shift the responsibility for more expenses to his shoulders. In my opinion, it makes sense that he should now be earning all his spending money. And when he starts driving, he should start paying at least some of his car expenses, if not all. In high school, I took over all my car expenses, and that may be your approach, or you may choose to have your teen cover just the gas, or something in between.

Your child's responsibility for managing his own budget should be growing as well, and this can be determined by his level of responsibility—or your comfort level with his responsibility. At some point during this age range, your teenager should take over management of all his spending—though you will still be providing a "salary" for some budget items.

Remember, in a few short years he will be away at college with total freedom to spend how he chooses. If he starts making decisions—including some mistakes—now, while he's under your roof, the consequences will probably be easier to handle. The stakes aren't as great, and the mistakes will be easier to correct.

The Stock Market
I wrote about this in greater detail in the previous chapter, and I suggest you continue what you started in the earlier years until either your children lose interest or they have greater interest and want to start using real money. When that happens, open an account for them with a small amount of money and begin showing them how. (Until your kids are 18, the account will need to be in your name or both of your names.) In the beginning, I would use an Internet account and get good advice from someone who's licensed to help in that way.

As with all financial advisors, make sure they don't have incentives to sell particular stocks. The financial group I was with was a good option for this—we owned our own Registered

Investment Advisory (RIA) service. However, keep in mind that RIA's are really set up to deal with accounts totaling $50,000 and higher. If you have smaller amounts to invest, you'll probably find it very hard to get much time from an advisor. I have put together some recommended resources and web sites to help you with investing at www.dadcents.com.

This investing account will be a great teaching tool, so your teenager can see how it works and the general costs of the account. Many online brokers have research tools to help you learn about the companies whose stock you are interested in purchasing. Once again, only use money you can afford to lose. Your goal will be to make money, but since no one can predict the market, be careful. Sometimes the stock market can bring negative returns comparable to a casino. Often, people only talk about the money they've won, so make sure your kids also hear about (and possibly experience) some losses in the market.

Credit

Credit is a dangerous tool that is very often misused. In the Bible, borrowing money is regarded as dangerous. Proverbs 22:7 says, "The rich rule over the poor, and the borrower is servant to the lender."

I would suggest that your kids never have any type of credit. I have often heard it said that borrowing robs God of the opportunity to show His love by providing for you. Author Randy Alcorn says the "Debt Mentality" involves:

- Believing you need more than God has given you the means to have.
- Believing God doesn't know best what your needs are.
- Believing God has failed to provide for your needs, forcing you to take matters into your hands.
- Presuming upon God that just because today's income

may be sufficient to make debt payments, so will tomorrow's.[18]

Credit card companies have exploited our country's problem with financial responsibility. M.P. Dunleavey of the *New York Times* writes,

"In the last couple of years, credit card companies have created cards that are a hybrid of credit, debit and gift cards—and the companies are marketing them squarely at teenagers."[19]

Cash cards allow parents to deposit money that is accessible by the card. The supposed benefits are that children can only spend the balance deposited on the card, and the statement allows parents to track spending. These are all great concepts, but those benefits are not worth the fact that your children are also being taught to use credit cards as a way of life, which is a dangerous mind set for teens and young adults. As with every area of life, we need to be aware of what habits and expectations our children are developing. According to Dunleavey,

"… some companies promote the [cash] cards as a step toward using credit cards. The parental information section on the MYplash [website] says: 'This will give your son/daughter a chance to get acquainted with a cash card prior to getting a credit card.'"[20]

One of the credit card companies even describes cash cards as a fiscal training tool! This subject is so very important to discuss with your kids. Upon entering college, they will receive numerous credit card applications, so knowing the dangers of credit is a must if they're going to be financially responsible.

Economic Concepts

As I'm sure you're aware, your children are in the stage of life that moves them closer and closer to leaving your home. The economic concepts that have been covered previously are opportunity cost, scarcity, savings, supply, demand, wants and needs. Instead of adding more concepts, I want to challenge you to help your teenage children come to a fuller knowledge of how these concepts affect their daily lives. If you aren't familiar with them, learn about them together with your child.

Knowing these terms can give your children an advantage over 98% of all other families in our country—and it's information that will definitely make a positive difference in their lives. Even at my daughters' young ages, they are beginning to see the reasons behind the specific ways we live out these concepts. I'll use the example of shopping for school clothing to demonstrate some ways to apply these concepts.

First, *savings* will remind you and your child to appreciate what God has provided; you'll both grasp the mind set of *scarcity*. If you are able to save, there is a greater chance of having resources to purchase additional clothing. This also reinforces the importance of *budgeting*. For example, if you have mentioned to your child several times during the past six months that he needs to save part of his monthly clothing budget for school clothes and he has failed to follow through, then getting new clothes in August cannot happen.

Next, choosing a shopping destination will be based partly on *scarcity*—limited resources despite unlimited wants and needs. While choosing where to look for and purchase clothes, a big factor is how much money your child has to spend. He will realize that he's in a position of scarcity, and money is scarcer for some than it is for others.

A note for those who have greater resources: Having plenty of money to buy what you want and need does not relieve you of the responsibility to be efficient and effective with the resources God has given you. Once your children understand scarcity, they will be much more likely to try outlet stores or wait and watch for seasonal clearance sales.

Supply and demand also comes into the picture. A mall

typically has clothes that are in higher demand and are higher in price. Outlet stores have clothes that are either overruns or a season out of date and are sold at a lower price. As you and your child grow in *contentment*, you will be well on your way to using supply and demand to your benefit.

Opportunity cost is used when deciding to purchase wants and/or needs. Remember, the opportunity cost is what must be given up (the next-best alternative) as a result of a decision. Given a limited amount of money, your kids must determine what they *need* and what they *want*. If they need underwear and socks, they will not be able to spend as much on shirts, blouses, jeans or shorts.

Application:

- Begin the next step in growing your children:

    1. Faithful – Talk to your children about specific ways God has been faithful to you. Do a Bible word study on the word "faithful" and discuss what you find. (On the Internet, you can use www.biblegateway.com or other Bible search sites.) Have them memorize one or more of the verses you find on faithfulness.
    2. Trustworthy – Do a word study on "trust" or "trustworthy" with your kids to see what the Bible says on the topic. Have them memorize one or more of the verses you find.
    3. Accountable – Through outside work opportunities and responsibilities, your child should be learning a lot about accountability.
    4. Foresight – Begin talking about college, with all the money responsibilities and challenges that will come their way.

5. Generosity – Take your kids to a local mission to serve. Giving to the needy is a command from God, and it will give your family a new perspective on how much He has blessed your family.

6. Shrewd – Teach your kids how to look for the lowest gas prices. Show them how to change the oil and either cut their own hair or find a very inexpensive option.

7. Effective – Getting the job done *well* will help your children grow their business. Being effective is a rare trait today.

8. Efficient – Encourage your kids to be self-employed if they have the ability to do so. From my experiences with this, I quickly learned that efficiency is a key to being successful. Your kids will learn to be efficient.

9. Disciplined – Have your kids start saving money for college. Month by month, show them how the money grows when they save even small amounts in a disciplined way.

10. Content – Have your kids help you budget the household funds. Show where the money goes and what has to happen to provide their salary.

11. Opportunity Cost, Scarcity, Savings, Supply & Demand, Wants vs. Needs – Begin to talk with your kids about the choices they make. Use some of the examples I gave above to show how economics affects us every day.

- Utilize the list of questions provided if you are considering buying your child a car or letting her drive one of your cars.

- Get an umbrella liability car insurance policy.

- Look up your state's driving laws regarding minors.

Last Chance

- Decide how much your kids will be responsible for covering their own expenses.

- Try out the stock market online.

"But be sure you live out the message and do not merely listen to it and so deceive yourselves." James 1:22

What would you do if you found a field with buried treasure? Would you be like the man in Jesus' illustration that was mentioned in an earlier chapter, and go to great lengths to get that field? Jesus is talking about the kingdom of heaven—we should be willing to do anything and give up anything to attain the prize of eternity with God.

Now, ask yourself this question: *How do I treat God's wisdom in the Bible?* Personally, I believe that pursuing godly wisdom goes hand-in-hand with accepting the gift of salvation. If your faith is important to you, then you'll be diligent about seeking to grow in your knowledge of God. So, I suppose there are two possible answers to my question: You would either implement the knowledge on a consistent basis, or you would not!

In the end, everything comes down to the big challenge: Will you follow through on what you've learned? Will you put the information and suggestions in this book to good use?

I'm willing to admit that a few of my suggestions might stretch what you're able to do in your current situation, or you might prefer a different approach (although I would still try to convince you of the wisdom of my approach). Still, I do feel confident that this book has given you some new ideas based on God's Word—or maybe I have reminded you of some things you have heard before. Whatever the case, as you have read this book, my desire is that you have thought, *I need to use that idea.* Or, *that could work in our family.*

This book has been written with much prayer—by myself and others. My greatest desire is to help change the way families utilize the money God has given them to manage, for the benefit of God's kingdom and the next generation. If I sell a million books and no one puts the concepts into practice with their children, then I have not really made a difference in this important area.

In James chapter 1, James makes a similar point to believers. He writes,

> But be sure you live out the message and do not merely listen to it and so deceive yourselves. For if someone merely listens to the message and does not live it out, he is like someone who gazes at his own face in a mirror. For he gazes at himself and then goes out and immediately forgets what sort of person he was. But the one who peers into the perfect law of liberty and fixes his attention there, and does not become a forgetful listener but one who lives it out—he will be blessed in what he does (22-25).

Dad, I want you and your family to be blessed by this book. I want you to be part of a bigger movement in our nation toward financial responsibility, led by the people of God in response to His Word. So please don't put this book down and immediately walk away and forget what you have read. Live it out! Start putting these concepts into practice with your kids.

The Challenge

If all of the suggestions seem overwhelming or they are too much to implement all at once, choose one or two ideas and start there. Over the weeks and months and years, add more concepts as you go. They really will make a difference.

God bless you and your family.

To help my children's future I commit to implementing:

-
-
-
-
-
-
-

Appendix A

Eternal Matters

I have written this book with the assumption that most readers are dads who have a saving relationship with Jesus Christ. (You probably noticed that along the way.) But for those who may not be in that group, I don't want to pass up this opportunity to talk about what really matters. I touched on this in the very first chapter, about building your foundation on the solid rock of Jesus Christ, but I also want to make sure you get the full picture.

No matter how you handle money management and teaching your kids about money, you have a choice to make every second of every day. Are you going to choose actions that are for God or against God?

Being fathers, we see examples of choices all the time by watching our children. Our third daughter, who has just turned four, tries very hard to keep up with her sisters and not get steam rolled in the process. A few years ago, she and I developed a game where she would sneak up behind and punch me, usually in the rear end, and then she'd run and I usually chased her. She would play the game for hours.

The problem was, over time she developed a pretty good little jab, and she didn't always use good judgment about when and with whom to use it. Sometimes, she would try to play that same "punch and run" game with her sisters or her cousins, and they didn't enjoy it much. They'd tell Mom or Dad, and Josie had to apologize. "Sowwy," she'd say, and then hug and kiss whomever was the latest punching bag. Then, after things cooled down and we thought it was over, she'd punch another victim! Looking at her cute little face, it was sometimes hard not to laugh while teaching her important lessons about being kind. She eventually grew out of it, and we hope she will continue to learn that she needs to make good choices consistently.

That's a kid-sized example, but it illustrates the truth behind our adult lives and concerns too. We also have daily choices about whether to obey and follow our Father, God, or pursue our own path. This is stated well by Elijah in 1 Kings 18. Elijah had arranged for a showdown between himself and 450 prophets of Baal, along with 400 prophets of Asherah. When King Ahab, the prophets of Baal, and the people of Israel arrived at Mt. Carmel, Elijah had a message for the people: "How long are you going to be paralyzed by indecision? If the Lord is the true God, then follow him, but if Baal is, follow him!" (v. 21).

You can read about the rest of what happened on that amazing day, but leading up to the big showdown, God wanted the people of Israel to *make a choice*. He still calls on each of us to make that choice. Choose God's way, or choose to follow the world or your own way. Make a choice!

I made that choice myself, but it took much longer than it should have. I was raised in a Bible-believing home and came to a saving knowledge of Jesus Christ at age six. Though I grew up in the church, I was ornery (as most boys are), and I challenged authority in my own ways. I was successful at hiding my failures and getting away with breaking the rules in subtle ways.

My parents were far from wealthy, and I learned to be very tight with my money. As I grew up and went through school,

I received an allowance and earned extra money, and I found that I had a knack for things related to money. The problem was that my good stewardship was not for God's kingdom—I was a good steward because I wanted things!

That continued when I reached the age when I moved out on my own; most of my choices were very selfish. Even after I graduated, married my beautiful bride and settled into the financial consulting profession, I played along with the "fake it until you make it" mentality, even while I kept attending church.

Then one day about eight years ago, God convicted me of the error of my ways. There was no moving mountaintop moment in my faith journey, but it became very clear to me that no matter how much money I had, being selfish did not mix with trying to be in God's will. The two are conflicting lifestyles, and trying to do both is a risky way to live. I was not taking big risks or living a wild lifestyle, but any lifestyle that doesn't put God first is risky; it's built on a shaky foundation and could come crashing down at any moment.

I am still very far from perfect, but I made that choice to follow Christ and put Him first. And though it's been a challenge for my wife and me, we have committed ourselves to seeing everything we have—even our children—as belonging to God. And He is continuing to teach me about how to be faithful to Him in all I do.

So, as you think about this choice, I have information that may help your decision. According to 1 Corinthians 7:23, "You were bought with a price..." The apostle Paul put it that way because, when we are without Christ, we are slaves to sin. If you are without Christ, it may not feel like you are a "slave" to sin, but the power of sin is influencing your daily decisions much more than you know, and leading you further from a life of hope and peace.

Dad Cents

Jesus' death on the cross paid the debt we could not pay and gave us the opportunity to be free from the power of sin in our lives. This freedom comes when we trust Him as our savior, through faith. Galatians 3:26 says, "For in Christ Jesus you are all sons of God through faith." Paul verifies this again in Galatians 4:7: "So you are no longer a slave but a son, and if you are a son, then you are also an heir through God." That isn't describing a mild feeling of acceptance or fondness that God has toward us, but a powerful and active love, like we feel toward our children. We are sons and heirs of God!

Once again, you have a choice to make, and this one will determine your eternal fate. You can become a child of God and start letting Him have control of the things you do every second of every day, in everything you do.

Joshua 24:15 says it well: "If you have no desire to worship the Lord, choose today whom you will worship, whether it be the gods whom your ancestors worshiped ... or the gods of the [people] in whose land you are living. But me and my family will worship the Lord!" Every day, we choose to give ourselves over to what our human nature desires (sin) or what God desires (obedience, which leads to life and peace).

Dad, what is motivating your actions? Do your actions show God's vision? Of course, none of us can live this life to perfection. We sin and that separates us from God. Jesus is the only human to ever live in our fallen world and not sin, and his sinless life makes him qualified to be the One who can bring us to God with our sins forgiven. In John 14:6, he said, "I am the way, and the truth, and the life. No one comes to the Father except through me." He gave his life for our sins, as the ultimate expression of God's great love for us. Then, he arose on the third day, demonstrating his power over death.

2 Peter 3:9 tells us that "[The Lord] is patient with you, not wanting anyone to perish, but everyone to come to repen-

tance." Out of love, He extended His offer of salvation to you and to your family. All you have to do is choose Him.

If you want to make that great choice and trust Jesus as your personal savior, say this prayer: **Jesus, I know that I have sinned and nothing I can do will earn my way to heaven. I understand that you died on the cross for my sins and I am depending on you alone for my salvation.**

If you prayed that for your first time, I would love to hear from you and help you begin your walk with Jesus. There's a lot more I would like to share with you about this choice. You can contact me at www.dadcents.com.

Appendix B

What do you know quiz

Here are the answers to the quiz in chapter 15. This quiz is also available on www.dadcents.com. The internet quiz is self grading.

1. By law there is a minimum liability limit on your car insurance. True | False

True. State law sets minimum liability limits.

2. If your golf clubs are stolen from your car, your car insurance covers the loss. True | False

False. Your house insurance covers the contents of your car.

3. An umbrella liability policy protects for damages over and above your car and house insurance. True | False

True. Liability umbrella policies provide liability coverage over the limits of your home and auto.

4. If your disability insurance is tax deductible, your benefit, if disabled, would be tax-free to you. True | False

False. The benefit would be taxed as income.

5. If you are disabled and have a group policy, your benefit could be lowered if you receive Social Security Disability Insurance. True | False

True. Most group policies have a stipulation that the benefit will decrease if the insured receives social disability benefits.

6. If you leave your place of employment, COBRA will allow you to continue your health insurance indefinitely. True | False

False. COBRA only extends your eligibility for 18 months but may be extended to 36 months if eligible.

7. Social Security is a good retirement plan. True | False

False. Most people who depend upon social security for their sole source of income live at or below to the poverty line.

8. If you have a will, your family members will not have to deal with going to probate court. True | False

False. A will guarantees a court date.

9. Term life insurance is intended to last forever. True | False

False. Term life insurance is only intended to last for a term as the name insinuates.

10. The death benefit of life insurance is tax-free. True | False

True. The death benefit of life insurance is tax free.

11. Interest received on savings accounts is tax-free. True | False

False. Interest on savings accounts is treated as current income.

12. Certificates of Deposit are very risky. True | False

False. CD's are insured and have guaranteed rates of return.

13. Tax deferred and tax deductible are the same. True | False

False. Tax deductible lowers your taxes now and you have no tax liability in the future. Tax deferred does not lower the tax now it postpones the tax to a later date.

14. Interest on your home mortgage is tax-deferred. True | False

False. It is tax deductible.

15. Money you place in your 401k is tax-deferred. True | False

True. When you begin to take income from your 401k you will be taxed at the then current income bracket.

16. Roth IRAs are tax-free if the money is withdrawn after 59½. True | False

True.

17. Money in an IRA is very liquid. True | False

False. Money in an IRA is taxed and penalized if you try to access it before 59 1/2. IRAs are considered very illiquid.

18. The tax penalty for withdrawing money from an IRA before 59 ½ is 15%. True | False

False. The tax penalty for early withdrawal is 10%.

19. If you own a bond you are acting as a lender to the issuing institution. True | False

True. When you own a bond you are loaning money to the issuer.

20. If you own stock in a company you own a part of that company. True | False

True. When you own stock you own a part of the company.

Notes:

1. Institute for American Values. The commission on thrift. *For a New thrift: confronting the Debt Culture. New York: Institute for American Values, 2008. p. 11.*

2. "shrewd" Microsoft® Encarta® http://encarta.msn.com © 1993-2004 Microsoft Corporation. All rights reserved.

3. Dictionary Andrew Clark and Andrew Oswald, "A Simple Statistical Method For Measuring How Life Events Affect Happiness." International Journal of Epidemiology 31.6 (2002), 1139-1144.

4. Andrew Oswald, cited in "Discover Data: The Cost of Contentment." Discover Magazine, 1 June 2003 <http://discovermagazine.com/2003/jun/breaknumbers>, 13 July 2007.

5. Thomas N. Robinson, MD, MPH, et.al., "Effects of Fast Food Branding on Young Children's Taste Preferences." Archives of Pediatrics & Adolescent Medicine 161.8 (Aug 2007), p. 792.

6. "Why Fruit Trees Fail to Bear." University of Rhode Island Landscape Horticulture Program, <http://www.uri.edu/ce/factsheets/sheets/fruittreesfail.html>, 24 July 2007. Adapted from Edmond L. Marrotte, Department of Plant Science, University of Connecticut.

7. Dave Simmons, Dad the Family Coach. Little Rock, AR: Dad the Family Shepherd, 1991, p. 70.

8. Simmons, Dad the Family Coach, p. 71.

9. "because" Microsoft® Encarta® http://encarta.msn.com © 1993-2004 Microsoft Corporation. All rights reserved.

10. Jonathan Clements, "Making Kids Money Savvy: Try These Four Financial Tricks." FiLife: Your Financial Lifeline. < http://www.filife.com/guides/making-kids-money-savvy-try-these-four-financial-tricks>, 14 September 2009.

11. "The Case for Economic Education." Center for Entrepreneurship and Economic Education, 16 November 2006. <http://www.umsl.edu/~econed/econ.htm>, 28 July 2007.

12. Joshua Kennon, "Your Guide to Investing for Beginners." about.com <http://beginnersinvest.about.com/cs/personalfinance1/a/051701a.htm>, 25 May 2007.

13. The National Council on Economic Education, "Why We Save," Lesson 8, Personal Finance Economics K-12. New York, NY: 1996, p. 1.

14. "Economics Basics: Demand and Supply." Investopedia. <http://www.investopedia.com/university/economics/economics3.asp>, 15 August 2007.

15. "luxury" Microsoft® Encarta® http://encarta.msn.com © 1993-2004 Microsoft Corporation. All rights reserved.

16. Maryland Legal Assistance Network. "How Changes in Maryland Law Affect Minor drivers." <http://www.marylandyouthlaw.com/driving/driving.htm>, 31 August 2007.

17. John H. Tyler, "Using State Child Labor Laws to Identify the Effect of School-Year Work on High School Achievement." Journal of Labor Economics, volume 21 (2003), pp. 381–408.

18. Randy Alcorn, "Debt: Who You Gonna Serve?" Eternal Perspective Ministries. <http://www.epm.org/artman2/publish/money_management/Debt_Who_You_Gonna_Serve.shtml>, 31 July 2009.

19. M. P. Dunleavey, "Cards Train Teenagers to Use Plastic." New York Times 25 August 2007: < http://www.nytimes.com/2007/08/25/business/25instincts.html>, 31 August 2007.

20. Dunleavey, "Cards Train Teenagers to Use Plastic."

...more help to be the dad you want to be

Conferences

Excel in your role as a **dad**. *Establish* a framework to strengthen your **marriage**. *Develop* benchmarks to assess your family's strengths and **growth** areas.

Presented by: Ken R Canfield, Ph. D.
Founded and served as the President & CEO of the National Center for Fathering from 1995-2005. Currently serves as the Executive Director of the Boone Center for the Family at Pepperdine University.

For information on hosting a Savvy Dads Conference and more information about the conference go to www.savvydads.net *or call at* 800-234-DADS